"*Creative Ways to Learn Ethics* provides readers with an imaginative, outside-the-box way to grapple with complex ethical issues. Dayna Guido shares a wide range of hands-on exercises designed to enhance professionals' grasp of ethics-related challenges. The book's user-friendly approach will appeal to practitioners who enjoy experiential learning. *Creative Ways to Learn Ethics* offers a useful supplement to prominent scholarly literature on professional ethics."

Frederic Reamer, PhD,
Professor, School of Social Work, Rhode Island College

"Dayna Guido's creative ideas bring ethics to life. She highlights important ethical issues with relevant, interesting, and engaging activities. Each chapter contains detailed descriptions of the activity, resources needed, and tips to adapt the activity based on audience or time constraints. This is an excellent resource for educators and trainers."

Tina M. Souders, PhD, JD, MSW, LCSW,
Clinical associate professor and director, Winston-Salem 3-Year MSW Program, University of North Carolina at Chapel Hill School of Social Work

Creative Ways to
Learn
Ethics

Creative Ways to Learn Ethics is an accessible, easy-to-read guide that compiles a variety of ethics trainings to help professionals stimulate their minds, relieve stress, and increase engagement and memory retention. The book uses a range of experiential and thought-provoking approaches, including contemplative exercises, expressive arts, games, and media. Each chapter contains objectives, detailed procedures, adaptations for different audiences, and handouts. Trainers, educators, clinicians, and other mental health professionals can use these exercises in various settings and modify them to meet the needs of their clients.

Dayna Guido, MSW, LCSW, ACSW, is a psychotherapist, clinical supervisor, consultant, educator, and trainer. She has a private practice in Asheville, North Carolina, and specializes in providing clinical supervision. She has been teaching graduate school for over 20 years as an adjunct instructor in clinical mental health counseling at Lenoir-Rhyne University, in the School of Social Work in the University of North Carolina at Chapel Hill, and in the Department of Social Work at Eastern Tennessee State University. Dayna is the co-author of *The Parental Tool Box for Parents and Clinicians*. She also serves on the NASW-NC Chapter Ethics Committee. She can be reached at daynaguido.com.

Creative Ways to
Learn
Ethics

*An Experiential Training Manual
for Helping Professionals*

Dayna Guido

Routledge
Taylor & Francis Group

NEW YORK AND LONDON

First published 2019
by Routledge
711 Third Avenue, New York, NY 10017

and by Routledge
2 Park Square, Milton Park, Abingdon, Oxon, OX14 4RN

Routledge is an imprint of the Taylor & Francis Group, an informa business

© 2019 Dayna Guido

Library of Congress Cataloging-in-Publication Data
Names: Guido, Dayna, author.
Title: Creative ways to learn ethics : an experiential training manual for
    helping professionals / Dayna Guido.
Description: New York, NY : Routledge, 2019. | Includes bibliographical
    references and index.
Identifiers: LCCN 2018031056 | ISBN 9781138587960
    (hardcover : alk. paper) | ISBN 9781138587977 (pbk. : alk. paper) |
    ISBN 9780429469664 (e-book)
Subjects: LCSH: Mental health personnel—Professional ethics. |
    Psychiatric ethics.
Classification: LCC RC455.2.E8 G847 2019 | DDC 174.2/9689—dc23
LC record available at https://lccn.loc.gov/2018031056

ISBN: 978-1-138-58796-0 (hbk)
ISBN: 978-1-138-58797-7 (pbk)
ISBN: 978-0-429-46966-4 (ebk)

Typeset in Garamond
by Apex CoVantage, LLC

To Jim who inspires me to explore the art of living
in a life affirming manner

Contents

Handouts

Acknowledgements

Gratitude goes to Ann Crews who once gave me feedback to share my creative ideas while providing supervision. Your comment helped open the door to expand my own use of self in clinical work.

Kelly Moore Spencer introduced me to the wonders of mask making and their metaphorical meanings. Thank you, Kelly, for unleashing in me a powerful way to study ethics.

My colleagues who have spent hours upon hours with me over the years discussing ethical dilemmas deserve much credit for the way I approach ethics at present. Thank you Julie Maccarin, Connie Hays, Jey Hiott, Jeanine Siler Jones, and Anne Bergeron for encouraging me, time and again, to choose the principled option. You have helped me to remain hopeful in the midst of complexity.

To Jason McKeown I am forever indebted for leading me to Routledge Publishing.

Anna Moore, my editor, and Nina Guttapalle, my editorial assistant, at Routledge/Taylor and Francis, have been exceedingly patient with my questions. Thank you both for providing me with support and guidance when I stumble.

Thank you, Lisa Mitchell. Your request for me to provide online training of Embodied Ethics stimulated a cascade of ideas. I woke up on my 60th birthday with the clear vision of this book based on your proffer. Your belief in the creative process in all of us is infectious.

Kerrie Fuenfhausen, Myra Jordan, and Tina Souders lifted me up with their encouragement after providing an advance reading. Thank you for easing my doubts on the value of this work.

I am, and continue to be, thankful for all my students and workshop participants who have wandered with me in the study of ethics. Your apt attention warms my heart and generates me to think of new and creative ways to teach.

Donna Limperes earns the award for always being there for me. From the beginning, literally and figuratively, Donna has been aware of all the exacting details. Thank you for making sure I am safe and allowing me to play with a free spirit.

Jim Guido has shared with me his love of words and definitions and for this I am forever grateful. Since we've met, he recognizes in me possibilities I only imagine. Jim's proficient use of the three voices (demander, stimulator, and soother) has kept me centered professionally and personally. Thank you for being by my side living our dreams.

Introduction

Sitting in the orientation to Jane Addams College of Social Work M.S.W. Program in 1982, I was moved and inspired by my first introduction to the NASW Code of Ethics. I remember the felt sense of finding my tribe as the Ethical Principles were displayed on the screen in front of us. These became the foundation upon which I would base my clinical practice to help others.

It quickly became evident from my own work experiences that a focus on ethics was critical to my professional growth and development. Faithfully, I attended ethics trainings and eagerly read all I could find on the subject. Often I was disappointed that during the trainings we were given little time to discuss at length, examine, and explore the topic with other professionals. Mainly we were taught ethics in a didactic manner, being instructed on what not to do in our practice. As a result of these experiences, I became committed to combining the experiential teaching of ethics with providing quality clinical supervision.

In my peer consultation groups and while providing individual and group supervision, I relished the opportunity to ponder and analyze ethical dilemmas. Applying various decision-making models for the specific situations presented brought clarity to the dilemma at hand. In actual clinical work the resolution frequently was not as simple as that provided in trainings.

It gradually became evident that experiential learning techniques allowed helping professionals to form a deeper understanding of the subject matter. This, in turn, increased their desire and ability to choose ethical behavior. I have found that a strong commitment to follow the ethical path develops during the process of decision making. Merely instructing intelligent professionals as to what to do, or not do, was often disregarded or seriously modified when training participants returned to their work environment. Discussing the nuances of a case and exploring options available for the clinician are essential for ethical conduct.

Following through on my commitment to make learning ethics interesting, I began using popular TV game shows, expressive arts activities, journaling, and film clips to teach ethics. The feedback from training participants and graduate students was overwhelmingly positive as they engaged in the learning process. *Creative Ways to Learn Ethics* is a selection of some trainings and classes I have taught over many years. Learning through playful or contemplative experiential activities is an effective means of stimulating the mind, and is an effective means of seeing problems in new ways, relieving stress, increasing engagement, and increasing memory retention.

There are four sections in the book: Using Games to Learn Ethics; Using Contemplative Exercises to Learn Ethics; Using Expressive Arts to Learn Ethics; and Using Media to Learn Ethics. The chapters are composed in the following manner:

- Objectives of Training
- Description of training
- Intended audience
- Approximate Time Suggested for Training
- Materials Suggested for Training required
- List of Handouts
- Adaptations
- Procedure
- Bibliography
- Handouts

The chapters are designed to be freestanding trainings or assembled together in a collection of trainings. Each training exercise may be shortened by limiting the activities, or extended by including additional material of the trainer's choice. Creative Ways to Learn Ethics is written for all helping professionals, educators, trainers, clinicians working with clients, supervisors, and other professionals.

Initially, my motivation for writing this book was to share some of my successful training techniques with helping professionals, educators and trainers. As I began the writing process, though, I recounted the times I also used the content with other professionals, individual clients, and client groups. Therefore, adaptations for other professionals and work with clients are included, when applicable, in each chapter (such as substituting the word morals for the word ethics). The material has proven to be easily adaptable for supervision groups and individual clinical supervision. The exercises can be completed as directed in the book, or the handouts and case scenarios used for discussion.

Individuals wanting to learn ethics on their own or in a group of two or three colleagues will also find *Creative Ways to Learn Ethics* a valuable resource. Most chapters can be modified for use without a formal trainer presenting the material. Browsing through the various exercises and handouts offers hours of ethical discussion.

It is recommended that trainers and educators familiarize themselves with all the material prior to presenting it. Additional lecture materials may be added by a trainer for specific client populations, situations, or treatment modalities. The benefit of this book is that it encourages the reader and participants to become more ethically aware in their responses. *Creative Ways to Learn Ethics* purposefully does not supply all the answers.

My intention is to share ideas for learning ethics in an experiential manner. I offer to each of you reading this book the opportunity to continue with the creative process. My invitation is for you to allow your own learning process to germinate and find new ways to explore and practice ethical conduct.

May you find joy in the pursuit of learning ethics.

Using Games to Learn Ethics

Section Summary:
Using Games to Learn Ethics

While ethics is a serious topic with significant consequences for both the helping professional and the client, training does not need to intimidate or put the participants to sleep by being dull. The intention in this section is to keep participants from being bored by creating a learning environment which includes laughter, curiosity, and enjoyment. Finding engaging ways to present ethics results in greater retention and willingness to review the material after the training.

The premise behind the chapters in this section, entitled *Using Games to Learn Ethics*, is that learning can be fun. Adult learning is enhanced when we offer the opportunity for participants to draw from their own experience, while challenging them in the ethical decision-making process and application of their Professional Code of Ethics. The use of games allows for greater participation and enjoyable interaction in the training.

The trainings are divided into three types of games: competition between individuals, competition between teams, and team-building games. Each chapter in this section is designed for thought-provoking discussion, ethical decision making, interaction amongst participants, play, and enjoyment.

Chapter 1

Going Once, Going Twice: The Ethical Values Auction starts with a contemplative exercise for participants to think through and prioritize their Ethical Values and Ethical Standards. Competition between individuals occurs during the Ethical Values Auction. Finally, participants are challenged to make ethical decisions based on their Ethical Values. Adapting the Auction for use with clients and groups is simple, which makes this training exercise suitable for a wider audience.

Chapter 2

Ethical Code Scavenger Hunt is a competition between individuals in the search for Ethical Standards. It offers an opportunity for stimulating discussion and processing ethical dilemmas.

Chapter 3

Ethics Trivia Game is a fast-paced competition between teams. Categories for the trivia questions include: confidentiality, diversity, documentation, technology, relationships with clients, competence, conflicts of interest, and research.

Chapter 4

Ethical Charades is a competition between teams. The game of Charades requires participants to think outside the box. Each round of the game is followed with the application of Ethical Standards to the book, TV show, movie, or song title. This is a training designed to include laughter, imagination, and fun while also increasing retention of Professional Ethical Codes.

Chapter 5

The Slippery Slope of Ethics is a board game which includes a competition between teams alongside team-building exercises.

Chapter 6

Building Ethical Organizations is an ideal training for team building on a full day retreat. The group is guided to develop their own game by the day's end.

Chapter 1

Going Once, Going Twice

The Ethical Values Auction

Objectives of Training

1. Identify ten Ethical Values which relate to various Professional Codes of Ethics
2. Prioritize Ethical Values in order of personal importance
3. Apply Ethical Values to an Ethical Case Dilemma using an applicable Professional Code of Ethics

Description of Training

The trainer serves as the Ethics Auctioneer in this invigorating training. Participants are led through an activity to prioritize their Ethical Values before beginning the bidding process of the auction using $1,000 in Ethical Value Bucks (provided in the handouts). Once all of the Ethical Values have been auctioned off, an ethical dilemma is introduced and participants use their acquired Ethical Values and Professional Code of Ethics to decide upon an ethical response. Large groups will need an Auctioneer for each group of ten people.

Intended Audience

Students, mental health professionals, other professionals, clients, and organizations
Suitable for small and large groups

Approximate Time Suggested for Training

3 hours

Materials Suggested for Training

Copy of an applicable Professional Code of Ethics for each participant
Handouts

List of Handouts

Ethical Values Handout (one for each participant)
Ethical Value Bucks (cut out, and ten Ethical Value Bucks given to each participant)
Ethical Value Tokens (one copy of the handout for each bidding group, cut out)
Ethical Case Dilemma Handout: The Case of Valuing Gender Identity
Blank cards (found in the Appendix)

Adaptations

Other professionals may substitute applicable Professional Values and an Ethical Case Scenario
For client groups substitute personal values for Ethical Values and a situational scenario for the Ethical Case Scenario
Organizations may substitute organizational values for Ethical Values and a situational scenario for the Ethical Case Scenario

Procedures

1. Introductions, and review the objectives of the training. (10 minutes)

2. Distribute the Ethical Values Handout to each participant. Discuss each of the Ethical Values as a large group, asking for definitions and examples of each. Clarify that each professional discipline has a Professional Code of Ethics, which sets standards and expectations of conduct and decision making based on Ethical Values and Ethical Principles. Ask for questions and comments before proceeding on to the activity. (15 minutes)

3. Explain that there will be silence during the next 10 minutes as participants individually complete the Ethical Values Handout. Allow enough time for each participant to complete the handout. (15 minutes)

4. Distribute $1,000 in Ethical Value Bucks (ten Value Bucks worth $100 each). Divide the participants into groups of up to ten people sitting together at a table or seated in a circle. There must be one (non-bidding) Auctioneer for each group. (5 minutes)

5. Explain the procedure of the auction. The Auctioneer will offer up each Ethical Value one at a time and start the bidding process at $100. The bids can only be made in increments of $100 using the Ethical Value Bucks. Participants only have ten Ethical Value Bucks at $100 each, so they must prioritize their bidding and spending. The Auctioneer will collect the Ethical Value Bucks from the highest bidder and issue the Ethical Value Token in return. In the case of a tie, the first person to call out the highest bid will be issued the Ethical Value Token. Ask for questions and clarifications needed. (5 minutes)

6. Proceed with the auction. (30 minutes)

7. Process with the entire group the following questions: (20 minutes)
   - What was your experience of prioritizing Ethical Values? What decision process did you use?
   - What was your experience during the auctioning? What decision process did you use?
   - For those of you who lost all bids and have no Ethical Values in your possession, what is your experience now?

8. Distribute the Ethical Case Dilemma Handout: The Case of Valuing Gender Identity, and read aloud the case.

   The Leading Edge Center is a residential treatment facility for adolescents with emotional and behavioral problems. There are separate cottages for male and female clients. Kelly Ling is a 16-year-old Asian, assigned female at birth client admitted to the female cottage. Kelly's parents, Mr. and Mrs. Ling, sought treatment for their daughter due to her lack of impulse control, irritability, feelings of worthlessness, binge eating, oppositional behavior, and excessive worrying. While conducting the initial clinical assessment with Kelly, the therapist learned that Kelly identifies as a male, which his/her parents have known about for 16 months. Kelly is adamant about wanting to be placed in the male cottage. When the therapist contacts Mr. and Mrs. Ling to discuss Kelly moving to the male cottage, they are insistent that Kelly is their daughter for whom they have medical and legal authority and they want her to receive treatment as a female in the female cottage. Mr. and Mrs. Ling are paying for Kelly's treatment.

One month into treatment (in the female cottage) Kelly admits to the therapist that he/she has been sneaking into bed with another client, Juanita Perez. Kelly states he/she will continue this behavior until moved to the male cottage. Juanita, a 14-year-old Mexican female, has often discussed in her therapy fears that she and her family will be deported since they do not have U.S. citizenship. Juanita admits she has been having sexual encounters with Kelly and does not want her parents to know. Juanita is on full scholarship at the Center.

Use the Ethical Value you possess and refer to your Professional Code of Ethics to answer the following questions:
- *If you are Kelly's individual therapist, what action(s) do you take?*
- *If you are Kelly's family therapist, what action(s) do you take?*
- *If you are Juanita's individual therapist, what action(s) do you take?*
- *If you are Juanita's family therapist, what action(s) do you take?*
- *If you are the Director of Leading Edge Center, what action(s) do you take?* (10 minutes to read and answer questions regarding the case)

9. Distribute to participants a copy of their applicable Professional Code of Ethics. Instruct them to identify specific Ethical Standards which demonstrate the application of the Ethical Value they possess (token) to the Ethical Case Dilemma and answer all the questions. In large group trainings with more than one auction, have participants gather with all others who possess the same Ethical Value Token to decide upon a course of action using this Ethical Value. Participants who do not have an Ethical Value Token will use the Ethical Value they prioritized as #1. (20 minutes)

10. Ask the possessor(s) of each Ethical Value to present to the entire group their responses to the Ethical Case Dilemma. (30 minutes)

11. Ask for Ethical Case Dilemmas from the participants and discuss as a large group how to apply their Professional Code of Ethics to the situation. (15 minutes)

12. Ask for final questions, comments, and closing statements. (5 minutes)

Bibliography

American Association for Marriage and Family Therapy. (2015). *Code of Ethics (PDF File)*. Retrieved from www.aamft.org/iMIS15/AAMFT/Content/Legal_Ethics/Code_of_Ethics

American Counseling Association. (2014). *ACA Code of Ethics*. Retrieved from www.counseling.org/knowledge-center/ethics

American Mental Health Counselor Association. (2015). *Code of Ethics*. Retrieved from http://connections.amhca.org/viewdocument/amhca-code-of-ethics

American Psychological Association. (2017). *Ethical Principles of Psychologists and Code of Conduct*. Retrieved from http://www.apa.org/ethics/code

Congress, E., Black, P., & Strom-Gottfried, K. (eds). (2009). *Teaching Social Work Values and Ethics: A Curriculum Resource*. Alexandria, VA: CSWE

Levitt, D. H., & Moorhead, H. J. H. (eds). (2013). *Values & Ethics in Counseling: Real-Life Decision Making*. New York, NY: Routledge

National Association of Social Work (N.A.S.W.). (2017). *Code of Ethics*. Retrieved from www.socialworkers.org/About/Ethics/Code-of-Ethics/Code-of-Ethics-English

National Board for Certified Counselors (N.B.C.C.). (2013). *Code of Ethics*. Retrieved from www.nbcc.org/Ethics/CodeOfEthics

Reamer, F. G. (2018). *Social Work Values and Ethics, Fifth Edition*. New York, NY: Columbia University Press

HANDOUT 1.1: ETHICAL VALUES HANDOUT

Prioritize the Ethical Values by placing a number from 1 (most important) to 10 (least important).

_____ Beneficence

_____ Competence

_____ Confidentiality

_____ Dignity and Worth of the Person

_____ Fidelity

_____ Honoring Diversity

_____ Integrity

_____ Non-Maleficence

_____ Social Justice

_____ Veracity

HANDOUT 1.1A: ETHICAL VALUE BUCKS HANDOUT

ETHICAL VALUE BUCK $ 100	ETHICAL VALUE BUCK $ 100
ETHICAL VALUE BUCK $ 100	ETHICAL VALUE BUCK $ 100
ETHICAL VALUE BUCK $ 100	ETHICAL VALUE BUCK $ 100
ETHICAL VALUE BUCK $ 100	ETHICAL VALUE BUCK $ 100
ETHICAL VALUE BUCK $ 100	ETHICAL VALUE BUCK $ 100

HANDOUT 1.1B: ETHICAL VALUE TOKENS HANDOUT

Beneficence	Competence
Confidentiality	Dignity & Worth of the Person
Fidelity	Honoring Diversity
Integrity	Non-Maleficence
Social Justice	Veracity

HANDOUT 1.2: ETHICAL CASE DILEMMA HANDOUT: THE CASE OF VALUING GENDER IDENTITY

The Leading Edge Center is a residential treatment facility for adolescents with emotional and behavioral problems. There are separate cottages for male and female clients. Kelly Ling is a 16-year-old Asian, assigned female at birth client admitted to the female cottage. Kelly's parents, Mr. and Mrs. Ling, sought treatment for their daughter due to her lack of impulse control, irritability, feelings of worthlessness, binge eating, oppositional behavior, and excessive worrying. While conducting the initial clinical assessment with Kelly, the therapist learned that Kelly identifies as a male, which his/her parents have known about for 16 months. Kelly is adamant about wanting to be placed in the male cottage. When the therapist contacts Mr. and Mrs. Ling to discuss Kelly moving to the male cottage, they are insistent that Kelly is their daughter for whom they have medical and legal authority and they want her to receive treatment as a female in the female cottage. Mr. and Mrs. Ling are paying for Kelly's treatment.

One month into treatment (in the female cottage) Kelly admits to the therapist that he/she has been sneaking into bed with another client, Juanita Perez. Kelly states he/she will continue this behavior until moved to the male cottage. Juanita, a 14-year-old Mexican female, has often discussed in her therapy fears that she and her family will be deported since they do not have U.S. citizenship. Juanita admits she has been having sexual encounters with Kelly and does not want her parents to know. Juanita is on full scholarship at the Center.

Use the Ethical Value you possess and refer to your Professional Code of Ethics to answer the following questions:

1. If you are Kelly's individual therapist, what action(s) do you take?
2. If you are Kelly's family therapist, what action(s) do you take?
3. If you are Juanita's individual therapist, what action(s) do you take?
4. If you are Juanita's family therapist, what action(s) do you take?
5. If you are the Director of Leading Edge Center, what action(s) do you take?

Chapter 2

Ethical Code Scavenger Hunt

Objectives of Training

1. Identify specific Ethical Standards in the applicable Professional Code of Ethics pertaining to responsibilities to clients and colleagues, including issues of diversity, fee setting, documentation, disclosures, and client rights.

Description of Training

The Ethical Code Scavenger Hunt is a lively, engaging, and thought provoking way to learn ethics. The trainer reads questions aloud from the Ethical Code Scavenger Hunt Questions Handout (included) and a timer is set for 2 minutes. Participants search through their applicable Professional Code of Ethics to locate as many of the specific Ethical Standards that pertain to the questions as they can. Answers are turned in and a discussion is led on the Ethical Standards. Participants are awarded Value Bucks (included in the Handouts) for correct answers.

Intended Audience

Students, mental health professionals, other professionals, and organizations
Suitable for individuals, small, and large groups

Approximate Time Suggested for Training

1 hour

Materials Suggested for Training

Copy of an applicable Professional Code of Ethics for each participant
Paper and pen for each participant
Prizes, if desired
Handouts

List of Handouts

Ethical Code Scavenger Hunt Questions Handout (one copy for the trainer)
Value Bucks Handout (copy and cut out at least 20 Value Bucks per participant)

Adaptations

To extend the length of the training, additional Ethical Code Scavenger Hunt Questions can be added
Other professionals may substitute an applicable Professional Code of Ethics and handouts

Procedures

1. Introductions, and review the objectives of the training. (5 minutes)
2. Distribute to participants a copy of their applicable Professional Code of Ethics. Explain that the trainer will read aloud one question from the Ethical Code Scavenger Hunt Questions Handout and set a timer for 2 minutes. Participants will locate as many of the specific Ethical Standards in their Professional Code of Ethics that pertain to the questions as they can, and write down the identifying number of the Ethical Standard(s). When the timer goes off, participants turn in their answers to the trainer. The trainer reads aloud the answers and allows for discussion. Participants will receive one Value Buck for each correct Ethical Standard identified. Note that each participant receives Value Bucks for every correct answer, so that for each round of questions multiple amounts of Value Bucks may be earned.
3. The trainer will continue to read aloud questions from the Ethical Code Scavenger Hunt Questions Handout and follow the procedure in #2 for the remainder of the time allocated for the training. The trainer can award prizes to the participant(s) earning the most Value Bucks, if desired.
4. Ask for final questions, comments, and closing statements. (5 minutes)

Bibliography

American Association for Marriage and Family Therapy. (2015). *Code of Ethics* (PDF File). Retrieved from www.aamft.org/iMIS15/AAMFT/Content/Legal_Ethics/Code_of_Ethics

American Counseling Association. (2014). *ACA Code of Ethics.* Retrieved from www.counseling.org/knowledge-center/ethics

American Mental Health Counselor Association. (2015). *Code of Ethics.* Retrieved from http://connections.amhca.org/viewdocument/amhca-code-of-ethics

American Psychological Association. (2017). *Ethical Principles of Psychologists and Code of Conduct.* Retrieved from www.apa.org/ethics/code/

Fisher, C. B. (2017). *Decoding the Ethics Code: A Practical Guide for Psychologists, Fourth Edition.* Thousand Oaks, CA: Sage Publications, Inc.

National Association of Social Work (N.A.S.W.). (2017). *Code of Ethics.* Retrieved from www.socialworkers.org/About/Ethics/Code-of-Ethics/Code-of-Ethics-English

National Board for Certified Counselors (N.B.C.C.). (2013). *Code of Ethics.* Retrieved from www.nbcc.org/Ethics/CodeOfEthics

Strom-Gottfried, K. (2016). *Straight Talk About Professional Ethics, Second Edition.* Oxford, UK: Oxford University Press

Sue, D. W., & Sue, D. (2016). *Counseling the Culturally Diverse: Theory and Practice, Seventh Edition.* New York, NY: John Wiley & Sons, Inc.

Voshel, E. H., & Wesala, A. (2015). 'Social Media & Social Work Ethics: Determining Best Practices in an Ambiguous Reality.' *Journal of Social Work Values & Ethics, 12:1,* 67–76

HANDOUT 2.1: ETHICAL CODE SCAVENGER HUNT QUESTIONS HANDOUT

1. What Ethical Standard(s) pertain to bartering with a client?
2. What Ethical Standard(s) pertain to diversity?
3. What Ethical Standard(s) pertain to terminating treatment if the client is no longer benefiting from services?
4. A client discloses their son-in-law is your child's teacher. What Ethical Standard(s) pertain to your decision of what to do?
5. A client is the head nurse in the assisted living facility that your parent recently moved into. What Ethical Standard(s) pertain to your decision of what to do?
6. A client refers a friend to your practice. What Ethical Standard(s) pertain to deciding whether you accept this referral?
7. You have a policy of sending a thank you to referral sources. A client refers someone to your practice. What Ethical Standard(s) pertain to whether you send your client a thank you for their referral?
8. A 17-year-old client requests you write their entrance letter to college. What Ethical Standard(s) pertain to your decision of what to do?
9. A discharged client still owes a substantial amount of their fee. The client requests a copy of their record and your colleague suggests you withhold their record until the fee is paid in full. What Ethical Standard(s) pertain to your decision?
10. What Ethical Standard(s) pertain to how long you maintain client records after discharge?
11. What Ethical Standard(s) pertain to discussing a client with your life partner?
12. What Ethical Standard(s) pertain to making referrals?
13. A client gifts you an engraved piece of jewelry. What Ethical Standard(s) pertain to your decision as to what to do in this situation?
14. A client has moved to another state and wants to continue to work with you. What Ethical Standard(s) pertain to your decision as to how to respond to their request?
15. An issue of client rights has been raised in your agency and your administrative supervisor tells you, "Those Ethical Standards of yours do not apply to this work setting." What Ethical Standard(s) pertain to your decision on what to do?
16. A client offers to design your website. What Ethical Standard(s) pertain to your decision as to how to respond to this offer?
17. An adult client asks you to provide treatment services for their elderly parent. What Ethical Standard(s) pertain to your decision as to how to respond to their request?

18. An adult client asks you to provide treatment services for their adolescent son. What Ethical Standard(s) pertain to your decision as to how to respond to their request?

19. A terminally ill client has disclosed their plan to hasten their own death. What Ethical Standard(s) pertain to any action you might take?

20. A client offers to provide a testimonial on your website. What Ethical Standard(s) pertain to your decision on whether to post this testimonial?

HANDOUT 2.1A: VALUE BUCKS HANDOUT

VALUE BUCK $ 1	VALUE BUCK $ 1
VALUE BUCK $ 1	VALUE BUCK $ 1
VALUE BUCK $ 1	VALUE BUCK $ 1
VALUE BUCK $ 1	VALUE BUCK $ 1
VALUE BUCK $ 1	VALUE BUCK $ 1

Chapter 3

Ethics Trivia Game

Objectives of Training

1. Identify Ethical Standards of competence in technology and diversity
2. Identify Ethical Standards of confidentiality and conflicts of interest

Description of Training

The Ethics Trivia Game is a fast-paced way to learn ethics. Participants are divided into teams to answer questions. Categories for the trivia questions include: confidentiality, diversity, documentation, technology, relationships with clients, competence, conflicts of interest, and research.

Intended Audience

Students, mental health professionals, other professionals, and organizations
Suistable for individuals, small, and large groups

Approximate Time Suggested for Training

1 hour

Materials Suggested for Training

Copy of an applicable Professional Code of Ethics for each participant
White board or flip chart and markers
Tape
Stopwatch
Prizes (optional)
Handouts

List of Handouts

Ethical Trivia Questions Handout
Ethical Trivia Tokens Handout #1 and #2 (one copy per team, tokens cut out, and placed in a bowl for each team)

Adaptations

To extend the length of the training, a discussion on each question can follow the correct answer
To extend the length of the training, additional questions can be developed by each team and challenged to the opposing team
Other professionals may substitute an applicable Professional Code of Ethics and handouts

Procedures

1. Introductions, and review the objectives of the training. (10 minutes)
2. Participants are divided into teams and each team is given a bowl containing the Ethical Trivia Tokens and copies of their applicable Professional Code of Ethics. The white board is divided into columns for each team. Teams are instructed to agree on a team name, which they write at the top of one of the columns on the white board. (5 minutes)
3. The team with the least combined work experience in years goes first. One team member from the first team picks an Ethical Trivia Token from their bowl. The trainer asks a trivia question pertaining to that category from the Ethical Trivia Questions Handout. The first team has 3 minutes to make a decision by referring to their Professional Code of Ethics and announce the answer to the trainer. If they answer the question correctly, the first team tapes their corresponding Ethical Trivia Token to the white board under their team name. If they answer incorrectly, the other team is given 1 minute to discuss and announce their answer. If the second team answers correctly, they tape their corresponding Ethical Trivia Token to their team column on the white board.
4. The game continues until one team has all their Ethical Trivia Tokens on the white board, or the allocated time for the training is up. Prizes can be awarded, if desired. (45 minutes)
5. Ask for final questions, comments, and closing statements. (5 minutes)

Bibliography

American Association for Marriage and Family Therapy. (2015). *Code of Ethics (PDF File)*. Retrieved from www.aamft.org/iMIS15/AAMFT/Content/Legal_Ethics/Code_of_Ethics

American Counseling Association. (2014). *ACA Code of Ethics*. Retrieved from www.counseling.org/knowledge-center/ethics

American Mental Health Counselor Association. (2015). *Code of Ethics*. Retrieved from http://connections.amhca.org/viewdocument/amhca-code-of-ethics

American Psychological Association. (2017). *Ethical Principles of Psychologists and Code of Conduct*. Retrieved from www.apa.org/ethics/code/

Devereaux, R. L., & Gottlieb, M. C. (2012). 'Record Keeping in the Cloud: Ethical Considerations.' *Professional Psychology: Research and Practice, 43,* 627–32

Farber, B. A. (2006). *Self-Disclosure in Psychotherapy*. New York, NY: The Guilford Press

Fisher, C. B. (2017). *Decoding the Ethics Code: A Practical Guide for Psychologists, Fourth Edition* Thousand Oaks, CA: Sage Publications, Inc.

Joint Task Force for the Development of Telepsychology Guidelines for Psychologists. (2013). 'Guidelines for the Practice of Telepsychology.' *American Psychologist, 68,* 791–800

Lannin, D. G., & Scott, N. A. (2013). 'Social Networking Ethics: Developing Best Practices for the New Small World.' *Professional Psychology: Research and Practice, 44,* 135–41

Luepker, E. T. (2012). *Record Keeping in Psychotherapy and Counseling: Protecting Confidentiality and the Professional Relationship, Second Edition*. New York, NY: Routledge

National Association of Social Work (N.A.S.W.). (2017). *Code of Ethics*. Retrieved from www.socialworkers.org/About/Ethics/Code-of-Ethics/Code-of-Ethics-English

National Board for Certified Counselors (N.B.C.C.). (2013). *Code of Ethics*. Retrieved from www.nbcc.org/Ethics/CodeOfEthics

Reamer, F. G. (2012). *Boundary Issues and Dual Relationships in the Human Services, Second Edition*. New York, NY: Columbia University Press

Sue, D. W., & Sue, D. (2016). *Counseling the Culturally Diverse: Theory and practice, Seventh Edition*. New York, NY: John Wiley & Sons, Inc.

Voshel, E. H., & Wesala, A. (2015). 'Social Media & Social Work Ethics: Determining Best Practices in an Ambiguous Reality.' *Journal of Social Work Values & Ethics, 12:1,* 67–76

Welfel, E. R. (2016). *Ethics in Counseling and Psychotherapy: Standards, Research, and Emerging Issues, Sixth Edition.* Boston, MA: Centage Learning

Zur, O. (2007). *Boundaries in Psychotherapy: Ethical and Clinical Explorations.* Washington, DC: American Psychological Association

Zur, O. (ed.) (2017). *Multiple Relationships in Psychotherapy and Counseling: Unavoidable, Common and Mandatory Dual Relations in Therapy.* New York, NY: Routledge

HANDOUT 3.1: ETHICAL TRIVIA QUESTIONS HANDOUT

Confidentiality

1. Does confidentiality end when a client dies? Answer the question and cite an Ethical Standard from your Professional Code of Ethics.
2. What action should be taken when a client with an incurable disease has an imminent plan to end their life? Answer the question and cite an Ethical Standard from your Professional Code of Ethics.

Diversity

1. You work as a clinician for a large, city Community Mental Health Center which has begun providing telemental health in rural counties. You have no training working with rural populations or in telemental health. Your supervisor assigns you three telemental health cases with an urgent need for you to begin immediately. What action should be taken? Answer the question and cite an Ethical Standard from your Professional Code of Ethics.
2. Your client is an undocumented immigrant and admits to physically abusing their six-year-old child. What action should be taken? Answer the question and cite an Ethical Standard from your Professional Code of Ethics.

Documentation

1. What action should be taken when you lose a client file? Answer the question and cite an Ethical Standard from your Professional Code of Ethics.
2. The attorney for one of the partners of a couple you saw in treatment two years ago subpoenas your clinical record for divorce proceedings. What action should be taken? Answer the question and cite an Ethical Standard from your Professional Code of Ethics.

Technology

1. You recently participated in a gun control demonstration and posted your opinion on social media. One of your clients saw you on the news and searched online successfully to read your social media post. The client came to their next session requesting a change in therapist. What action should be taken? Answer the question and cite an Ethical Standard from your Professional Code of Ethics.

2. A potential client discovers your website and requests an appointment via email. The client's name sounds vaguely familiar and you want to find out more about the person. What action should be taken? Answer the question and cite an Ethical Standard from your Professional Code of Ethics.

Relationships with Clients

1. Your client moves into the house next door to you. What action should be taken? Answer the question and cite an Ethical Standard from your Professional Code of Ethics.
2. You are a licensed psychotherapist and recently obtained a ministry certificate online to perform wedding ceremonies. Your individual psychotherapy client asks you to perform his wedding. What action should be taken? Answer the question and cite an Ethical Standard from your Professional Code of Ethics.

Competence

1. After treating an anxious client for six months, your client reveals details of childhood trauma. You are not trained in trauma-informed treatment and want to make a referral to another professional. Your client begs to remain working with you. What action do you take? Answer the question and cite an Ethical Standard from your Professional Code of Ethics.
2. You attend an introductory training at a one-hour Lunch and Learn on a specific treatment model. This treatment model offers certification only after extensive training. One of your colleagues is in attendance at the same Lunch and Learn. Later that evening you notice that this colleague has posted on a professional social media site stating they are now providing treatment in the specific model presented at the Lunch and Learn. What action should be taken? Answer the question and cite an Ethical Standard from your Professional Code of Ethics.

Conflicts of interest

1. Is using a collection agency to collect unpaid fees an invasion of client privacy? Answer the question and cite an Ethical Standard from your Professional Code of Ethics.

2. A past client is hired as the Information and Technology Director at your agency and has access to all computer records. What action should be taken? Answer the question and cite an Ethical Standard from your Professional Code of Ethics.

Research

1. During an interview gathering research data, the client becomes emotionally distressed. What action should be taken? Answer the question and cite an Ethical Standard from your Professional Code of Ethics.

2. You work for an organization which has received private funds for extending outreach programing to the LGBTQIA community. Your supervisor is on the verge of publishing a major research project which unexpectedly needs additional funding to complete. Your supervisor decides to use the private funds allocated for the outreach services to finance the research project. What action should be taken? Answer the question and an Ethical Standard from your Professional Code of Ethics.

HANDOUT 3.1A: ETHICAL TRIVIA TOKENS HANDOUT #1

Confidentiality

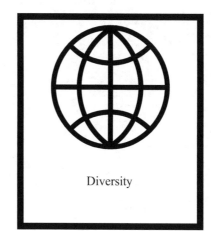

Diversity

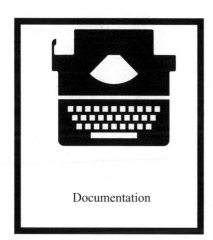

Documentation

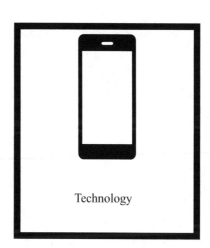

Technology

HANDOUT 3.1B: ETHICAL TRIVIA TOKENS HANDOUT #2

Relationships
with
clients

Competence

Conflicts
of
interest

Research

Chapter 4

Ethical Charades

Objectives of Training

1. Apply relevant Ethical Standards to ethical references

Description of Training

This interactive ethics training exercise is called *Charades*. Participants divide into teams and pantomime ethical references to their team members, pulled from an Ethical Charades Card deck (included). Teams get points for correct guesses and additional points for correctly identifying Ethical Codes and Standards corresponding to each title.

Intended Audience

Students, mental health professionals, other professionals, and organizations
Suitable for individuals, small, and large groups

Approximate Time Suggested for Training

1 hour

Materials Suggested for Training

Copy of an applicable Professional Code of Ethics for each participant
Stopwatch
White board or flip chart
Prizes (optional)
Handouts

List of Handouts

Ethical Charades Cards #1, #2, and #3 (cut out each card and place in a bowl)
Additional blank cards (in Appendix), if needed

Adaptations

To extend the training time additional blank cards are provided in the Appendix for teams to create their own titles related to ethics. These cards will be picked by the opposite team to continue the game of Charades.
Other professionals may substitute an applicable Professional Code of Ethics

Procedures

1. Divide participants into teams and explain the rules of Charades. The teams can choose their team name. The trainer or their designee will write the team names on the white board. Each time points are scored they will be added to the appropriate team total. (5 minutes)

2. Distribute copies of the applicable Professional Code of Ethics to each participant.

3. Choose a team to go first and one member from that team picks an Ethical Charades Card which has the title to a book, film, TV show, or song (the title only is based on ethical references) and pantomime it to their team members. The team gets two points for guessing correctly within 3 minutes. If the first team cannot guess correctly within the time frame, the second team has a member pantomime the same card to their team. The second team gets 2 more minutes to guess correctly and earn one point. If there are more than two teams the trainer can adjust the point spread as needed to accommodate the number of teams playing the game.

4. Teams are then allowed 5 minutes to identify and write down specific Ethical Codes that pertain to the title. At the end of the five minutes ask the teams to hand in the written responses listing the specific Professional Code of Ethics, the relevant Ethical Standard, and the corresponding number of the Ethical Standard. The trainer reads out the responses and awards the points. For each appropriate response the team earns two points which are added to the team total. Teams can have the same responses and earn points.

5. After each round discuss with participants any ethical dilemmas related to the Ethical Standards specified. This will allow for questions and teaching on various ethical issues.

6. Proceed in this same manner until all of the Ethical Charade Cards have been used or the time for the training is almost over.

7. Ask for final questions, comments, and closing statements. (5 minutes)

Bibliography

American Association for Marriage and Family Therapy. (2015). *Code of Ethics* (PDF File). Retrieved from www.aamft.org/iMIS15/AAMFT/Content/Legal_Ethics/Code_of_Ethics

American Counseling Association. (2014). *ACA Code of Ethics.* Retrieved from www.counseling.org/knowledge-center/ethics

American Mental Health Counselor Association. (2015). *Code of Ethics.* Retrieved from http://connections.amhca.org/viewdocument/amhca-code-of-ethics

American Psychological Association. (2017). *Ethical Principles of Psychologists and Code of Conduct.* Retrieved from www.apa.org/ethics/code

National Association of Social Work (N.A.S.W.). (2017). *Code of Ethics.* Retrieved from www.socialworkers.org/About/Ethics/Code-of-Ethics/Code-of-Ethics-English

National Board for Certified Counselors (N.B.C.C.). (2013). *Code of Ethics.* Retrieved from www.nbcc.org/Ethics/CodeOfEthics

HANDOUT 4.1A: ETHICAL CHARADE CARDS HANDOUT #1

Kitchen Confidential
book/TV show

True Justice
TV show

Do the Right Thing
movie

Sophie's Choice
book/movie

Consenting Adults
movie

Help
song/book/movie

Law & Order
TV show

Fifty Shades of Gray
book/movie

True Lies
movie/song

L.A. Confidential
film/song

HANDOUT 4.1B: ETHICAL CHARADE CARDS HANDOUT #2

All Along the Watchtower song	**The DaVinci Code** book/movie
Liar Liar song/movie	**Private** book
Code Girls book	**Everybody Wants to Rule the World** song
Rules of Engagement TV show/movie	**The Outer Limits** TV show
Take it to the Limit song	**Creative Ways to Learn Ethics** book

HANDOUT 4.1C: ETHICAL CHARADE CARDS HANDOUT #3

Judgement Day movie/book	**License to Kill** book/movie/song
Portnoy's Complaint book/movie	**I Want to Hold Your Hand** song
Respect song	**Minority Report** movie/book/TV show
Conflict of Interest movie	**You Can't Always Get What You Want** song
Cross the Line song/book	**Don't Think Twice, It's All Right** song

Chapter 5

The Slippery Slope of Ethics

Objectives of Training

1. Apply ethical problem-solving methods to case dilemmas
2. Examine choices relevant to ethical dilemmas

Description of Training

The Slippery Slope of Ethics is a board game for 6–24 people with opportunities to work in teams while problem-solving ethical dilemmas. This game is developed to allow for ample discussion of each dilemma. Two of the teams represent professionals abiding by Ethical Codes who are competing to reach the peak of the Ethical Mountaintop first. The third team represents the Ethics Board and decides whether the two competing teams can proceed up the Ethical Mountaintop based on their answers to the ethical dilemmas.

Intended Audience

Students, mental health professionals, other professionals, and organizations Suitable for groups of 6–24

Approximate Time Suggested for Training

2 hours

Materials Suggested for Training

Copy of an applicable Professional Code of Ethics for each participant
The Slippery Slope of Ethics Game available at daynaguido.com

Adaptations

Additional cards and instructions are provided in the game for other professionals and organizations to develop suitable ethical dilemmas.

Procedures

1. Participants are divided into three teams and given their first set of instructions.

2. Two of the teams represent professionals abiding by Ethical Codes competing to reach the peak of the Ethical Mountaintop first. They are instructed to create additional Ethical Dilemma Cards to place on the game board.

3. The third team represents the Ethics Board and creates additional Take a Hike Cards (such as: You attend a diversity training, move ahead two spaces) to place on the game board.

4. The game board is designed with a trail leading up to the Ethical Mountaintop. The two competing teams take turns to move up and down the mountain by answering the game cards related to ethical dilemmas.

5. The Ethics Board team decides whether the two competing teams can proceed up the Ethical Mountaintop, or whether they need to make amends based on their answers to the ethical dilemmas.

6. After each decision is made the entire group discusses the dilemma thoroughly.

7. Blank cards are included with the game allowing participants to create additional ethical dilemmas suited to their settings. The official game, *The Slippery Slope of Ethics*, can also be purchased at daynaguido.com.

Bibliography

American Association for Marriage and Family Therapy. (2015). *Code of Ethics (PDF File)*. Retrieved from www.aamft.org/iMIS15/AAMFT/Content/Legal_Ethics/Code_of_Ethics

American Counseling Association. (2014). *ACA Code of Ethics*. Retrieved from www.counseling.org/knowledge-center/ethics

American Mental Health Counselor Association. (2015). *Code of Ethics*. Retrieved from http://connections.amhca.org/viewdocument/amhca-code-of-ethics

American Psychological Association. (2017). *Ethical principles of psychologists and code of conduct*. Retrieved from www.apa.org/ethics/code

National Association of Social Work (N.A.S.W.). (2017). *Code of Ethics*. Retrieved from www.socialworkers.org/About/Ethics/Code-of-Ethics/Code-of-Ethics-English

National Board for Certified Counselors (N.B.C.C.). (2013). *Code of Ethics*. Retrieved from www.nbcc.org/Ethics/CodeOfEthics

Chapter 6

Building Ethical Organizations

Objectives of Training

1. Describe Ethical Values and Ethical Principles in an organization's Mission Statement
2. Identify possible social diversity issues within an organization
3. Describe ethical decision-making processes within an organization

Description of Training

This full-day training is specifically designed to enable organizations to discuss their ethical work environment. It is an ideal way to obtain training hours during a work retreat, allowing for organizational self-assessment and appraisal. Team-building exercises lead participants from the same organization to develop and play a game pertaining to ethics. Opportunities to examine the organizational Mission Statement, Ethical Values and Ethical Principles, and social diversity considerations are provided. Ethical dilemmas and decision-making processes are built into the development of the game.

Intended Audience

Students, mental health professionals, other professionals, and organizations
Suitable for small and large groups

Approximate Time Suggested for Training

5–6 hours

Materials Suggested for Training

Copy of an applicable Professional Code of Ethics for each participant

Flip chart, markers, and masking tape

Package of 100 multicolored 3" x 5" index cards

Pair of dice

Five small items to be used as game pieces

Large poster board

Mission Statement of the organization written out on a piece of flip chart paper and taped to a wall in the training room

Adaptations

To shorten the length of the training, omit the development and playing of the ethics game

Students may substitute the school's Mission Statement for the organization's Mission Statement

Procedures

1. Introductions, and review the objectives of the training. (10 minutes)

2. Distribute to participants a copy of their applicable Professional Code of Ethics. Review the organization's Mission Statement which should be posted on the wall. Ask participants to identify Ethical Values and Ethical Principles that are important to the organization. As the Ethical Values and Ethical Principles are named, ask one participant to write them on the flip chart. (15 minutes)

3. As an entire group, examine the Ethical Values and Ethical Principles posted on the flip chart and organize them into a maximum of five conceptual categories. This is a subjective group experience, necessitating discussion and decision making. Ask one participant to write each conceptual category (with all of the combining Ethical Values and Ethical Principles listed underneath) at the top of separate pieces of flip chart paper. Tape each of these conceptual categories on the wall. (15 minutes)

4. Instruct participants to divide into five groups (or as many groups as there are conceptual categories). Allow time for the groups to gather together and move their chairs to form circles. If there are not enough people to form five groups, assign multiple categories to each group. (5 minutes)

5. Assign each group one of the five conceptual categories with the instruction to write a sentence describing how the organization assures that the Ethical Values and Ethical Principles in this conceptual category are observed. This, too, is a subjective group experience necessitating discussion and decision making. Ask one participant from each of the five groups to write the sentence on the corresponding conceptual category flip chart paper taped to the wall. (15 minutes)

6. Gather the entire group together and review the sentences added to the conceptual categories. As the sentences are read aloud, allow for discussion on the process of developing the sentence from the small group; ask for thoughts, comments, and questions from the large group. (15 minutes)

7. Ask participants to look at each of the conceptual categories and sentences, examining them from a cultural awareness and social diversity perspective. Ask the following questions for each conceptual category and sentence. (20 minutes)
   - *Is there evidence of prejudice or judgment?*
   - *Is there evidence of racism, agism, sexism, or stereotyping?*
   - *Is there evidence of oppression or discrimination?*
   - *Is there evidence of social, political, or institutional barriers?*
   - *Are there changes the entire group wants to make to this sentence?*

8. Explain that the time has come for the entire group to apply all of the information posted around the room on the flip chart paper and develop a game for the group to play. Possibilities include a board game, card game, or game show. Describe the materials supplied to create this game. Lead the group in a discussion and decision-making process on how they want to proceed with developing this game. Remind them that the purpose of this game should pertain to ethics. The following should be included in the game: (5 minutes)
   - *Organizational Mission Statement*
   - *Ethical Dilemmas with Decision-Making Opportunities*
   - *Ethical Values and Ethical Principles*
   - *Cultural Awareness and Social Diversity Considerations*

9. It is recommended that the trainer provides realistic time frames on accomplishing the following tasks, depending on the overall training time constraints. (Suggestion time frames are provided.)
   - *Agreement on the type of game (15 minutes)*
   - *Division of labor – each group has a particular assignment to accomplish (30 minutes to one hour)*
   - *Playing the game (30 minutes to one hour)*
   - *Review of the game and the ethical issues presented (15 minutes)*
   - *Review of the decision-making processes employed throughout the entire day pertaining to ethics (15 minutes)*

10. Ask for final questions, comments, and closing statements. (5 minutes)

Bibliography

American Association for Marriage and Family Therapy. (2015). *Code of Ethics (PDF File)*. Retrieved from www.aamft.org/iMIS15/AAMFT/Content/ Legal_Ethics/Code_of_Ethics

American Counseling Association. (2014). *ACA Code of Ethics*. Retrieved from www.counseling.org/knowledge-center/ethics

American Mental Health Counselor Association. (2015). *Code of Ethics*. Retrieved from http://connections.amhca.org/viewdocument/amhca-code-of-ethics

American Psychological Association. (2017). *Ethical Principles of Psychologists and Code of Conduct*. Retrieved from www.apa.org/ethics/code/

Corey, G., Corey, M., & Corey, C. (2018). *Issues and Ethics in the Helping Professions, Tenth Edition*. Stamford, CT: Brooks/Cole Cengage Learning

Levitt, D. H., & Moorhead, H. J. H. (eds) (2013). *Values & Ethics in Counseling: Real-Life Decision Making*. New York, NY: Routledge

National Association of Social Work (N.A.S.W.). (2017). *Code of Ethics*. Retrieved from www.socialworkers.org/About/Ethics/Code-of-Ethics/ Code-of-Ethics-English

National Board for Certified Counselors (N.B.C.C.). (2013). *Code of Ethics*. Retrieved from www.nbcc.org/Ethics/CodeOfEthics

Pope, K. S., & Vasquez, M. J. (2016). *Ethics in Psychotherapy and Counseling: A Practical Guide*. Hoboken, NJ: John Wiley & Sons, Inc.

Tribe, R., & Morrissey, J. (eds) (2015). *Handbook of Professional and Ethical Practice for Psychologists, Counsellors and Psychotherapists, Second Edition*. New York, NY: Routledge

Welfel, E. R. (2016). *Ethics in Counseling and Psychotherapy: Standards, Research, and Emerging Issues, Sixth Edition*. Boston, MA: Centage Learning

Using Contemplative Exercises to Learn Ethics

Section Summary: Using Contemplative Exercises to Learn Ethics

By its very nature, ethics encourages one to think, ponder, reflect, and consider. This section, entitled *Using Contemplative Exercises to Learn Ethics*, provides ample opportunity for helping professionals to examine their Professional Code of Ethics and formulate their own actions based on ethical decision making.

Learning can be accomplished in these trainings by any size group, or an individual on their own. Contemplation enhances our learning process by challenging us to think through the options and make a decision. Guided imagery, journal exercises, Action Plan development, and discussion opportunities are offered in the context of contemplating ethics.

Chapter 7

Writing Your Ethical Eulogy guides participants to use contemplative exercises to think, write, engage in a guided imagery, and discuss their thoughts with others. They come away from the training having written an Ideal Ethical Identity Mission Statement and Action Plan.

Chapter 8

Ethics on a Cloudy Day: Developing Action Plans for Technologically Cloudy Questions stimulates participants to think about technology and how it relates to their practice of ethics. Through the use of small groups, participants develop Ethical Action Plans. An added bonus feature of this chapter is the list of 30 questions related to technology and ethics, which can be used independently.

Chapter 9

Supervisory Ethics combines written exercises with discussion to explore supervisory boundaries; remote and electronic supervision; evaluation of supervisees; and responses to ethical supervision dilemmas. The four different handouts are designed for supervisors to complete individually, making this an ideal chapter to use for independent learning.

Chapter 10

Developing Ethical Resources guides participants through their own self-discovery process, which culminates in writing an Ethical Resource Action Plan. The intention of the questions in the handouts is to assist helping professionals to stimulate self-reflection.

Chapter 11

Developing Ethical Rituals combines both contemplative and expressive arts exercises in a thought-provoking manner. It is a quick one-hour training which opens the mind to consider ethics in a new light.

Chapter 7

Writing Your Ethical Eulogy

Objectives of Training

1. Develop an Ethical Identity Mission Statement
2. Identify necessary components of a Professional Will

Description of Training

Writing Your Ethical Eulogy is a training which allows participants to thoughtfully immerse themselves in exercises designed to create an ideal professional ethical identity. Using guided imagery, journal exercises, and discussion participants are escorted through a process to write their ethical eulogy and then develop an ideal Ethical Identity Mission Statement and Action Plan. Finally, participants will learn the important components to include in a Professional Will.

Intended Audience

Students, mental health professionals, other professionals, clients, and organizations
Suitable for individuals, small, and large groups

Approximate Time Suggested for Training

2 hours

Materials Suggested for Training

Copy of an applicable Professional Code of Ethics for each participant
Paper and pens (participants are encouraged to bring their own journals)
Handouts

List of Handouts

Writing Your Ethical Eulogy Handout
Ethical Identity Mission Statement Handout
Ethical Identity Mission Statement Action Plan Handout
Professional Will Handout

Adaptations

Other professionals may substitute appropriate wording on the Professional
Will Handout
For clients, modify handouts to fit client specific issues

Procedures

1. Introductions, and review the objectives of the training. (10 minutes)
2. Invite participants to sit comfortably in their chairs with their feet on the floor and their hands gently relaxing in their laps. Explain that the following guided imagery will focus on participants visualizing how their ethical conduct might be recalled by others at the end of their career or life. Read the following guided imagery out loud, very slowly. (10 minutes)

   - *Relax comfortably in your chair with your feet on the floor. Breathe deeply and feel grounded and safe in your surroundings. If you are comfortable, close your eyes gently. Imagine you are witnessing a retirement gathering in your honor, your end-of-life ceremony, or a memorial service for you. Take some time to set the scene of your choosing. Where will this be held?*
   - *There will be words spoken about how you demonstrated ethical conduct during your career. Imagine if you want this event to take place upon your retirement, near the end of your life, or after you have died.*
   - *Who will be in attendance?*
   - *Who will speak?*
   - *Do you want one person, a few, or many people to speak?*
   - *Do you want any form of media included such as music, video, or a pictorial slide presentation? What are those specifics?*
   - *Play out the details in your mind, imaging you are an observer of this scene. Take your time to imagine the details.*
   - *What do you want the speakers to say about your ethical conduct over the course of your career?*
   - *Does this include Ethical Values, contributions you have made to the field of ethics, or specific situations in which you made wise, ethical decisions?*
   - *When you are ready, open your eyes and breath gently.*

3. Instruct participants to write down all that they can remember of the guided imagery. Allow enough time for each participant to write down their experience. (10 minutes)
4. Ask participants if anyone wants to briefly share the words or recollections they visualized in the guided imagery. Ask the group if they can identify specifics from their Professional Code of Ethics which would pertain to the words or recollections. If the group is large, participants can be paired in twos to share and discuss. (10 minutes)

5. Explain that there will be silence as participants individually complete the Writing Your Ethical Eulogy Handout. Distribute the handout to each participant and instruct them to answer the questions on the form, or in their own journals. Allow enough time for each participant to complete the five questions. The trainer can circulate around the room and provide support and guidance as needed. (15 minutes)

6. Discuss with the group how they chose certain Ethical Values and Ethical Principles. Discuss if their answers as to the words spoken by colleagues, supervisors, and clients were different or similar. (5 minutes)

7. Explain that a mission statement defines one's Ethical Values, provides clarity for making ethical decisions, and guides action. Explain that there will be silence again as participants individually complete the Ethical Identity Mission Statement Handout. Distribute the handout to each participant and instruct them to develop their Ethical Identity Mission Statement on the form or in their own journals. They can choose to write in sentences or bullet points, whichever format they prefer. Explain that a mission statement often takes much deliberation and introspection, completed over many days or even months. This is merely the start of developing their Ethical Identity Mission Statement which they can continue working on after the training ends. The trainer can circulate around the room and provide support and guidance as needed. (15 minutes)

8. Distribute to participants the Ethical Identity Mission Statement Action Plan Handout. Review the questions in the handout and instruct them to write their answers on the handout or in their journals. (10 minutes)

9. Instruct participants to find a partner with whom to share and discuss their Ethical Identity Mission Statement Action Plan, reminding them that this is a work in progress. (10 minutes)

10. Ask participants if anyone wants to share briefly their experience with this exercise, what they have learned from it, and how they plan on incorporating it into their professional lives. (10 minutes)

11. Distribute to participants the Professional Will Handout. Explain the recommendation by ethics experts that all licensed clinicians need to have a Professional Will to plan for what happens if they become incapacitated or die while still working. Review the handout and discuss. (10 minutes)

12. Ask for final questions, comments, and closing statements. (5 minutes)

Bibliography

Covey, S. R. (2004). *The 7 Habits of Highly Effective People.* New York, NY: Simon and Schuster

National Association of Social Work (N.A.S.W.). *The Professional Will.* Retrieved from www.naswassurance.org/malpractice/malpractice-tips/the-professional-will/

Pope, K. S., & Vasquez, M. J. (2016). *Ethics in Psychotherapy and Counseling: A Practical Guide.* Hoboken, NJ: John Wiley & Sons, Inc.

Reamer, F. G. (August 2013). 'Planning Ahead - Drafting a Professional Will.' *Social Work Today.* Retrieved from www.socialworktoday.com/news/eoe_081213.shtml

Zur Intstitute. *The Professional Will.* Retrieved from www.zurinstitute.com/wills_clinicalupdate.html

HANDOUT 7.1: WRITING YOUR ETHICAL EULOGY HANDOUT

1. Look over your Professional Code of Ethics and list the Ethical Values and Ethical Principles you want to be remembered for upholding during your career.

2. How do you want your colleagues to describe you?

3. How do you want your supervisors to describe you?

4. How do you want your clients to describe you?

5. What kind of legacy do you want to leave?

HANDOUT 7.2: ETHICAL IDENTITY MISSION STATEMENT HANDOUT

A mission statement defines one's Ethical Values, provides clarity for making ethical decisions, and guides conduct. Consider your responses on the Ethical Eulogy Handout and put into words a complete and concise statement of your ideal ethical identity.

HANDOUT 7.3: ETHICAL IDENTITY MISSION STATEMENT ACTION PLAN HANDOUT

1. These are actions I can take in the next week to work towards realizing my desired ethical identity.

2. These are actions I can take in the next month to work towards realizing my desired ethical identity.

3. These are actions I can take in the next year to keep me on my path to achieve my desired ethical identity.

4. These are actions I can take in the next five years to provide direction for my desired ethical identity.

HANDOUT 7.4: PROFESSIONAL WILL HANDOUT

1. Choose a Healthcare Professional Executor who will assume responsibility in case of your incapacitation or death. It is wise to choose a back up designee as well.

2. Meet with your Healthcare Professional Executor to obtain their consent to fulfill this role and to explain the details of your Professional Will.

3. Provide written instructions to your Healthcare Professional Executor detailing the following information:

   Location of keys to office, all doors, and filing cabinets

   Location of all (present and past) client records (clinical, billing, and financial)

   Location of schedule, appointment book, or device

   Access to all professional contact information

   Preference for clients' notification and privacy

   Access to all electronic usernames and passwords

4. Your Professional Will should detail the following information:

   Name and contact of Healthcare Professional Executor

   All the information detailed in the written instructions to the Executor (above)

   Professional liability insurance information

   Names of colleagues who should be notified

   Names of other professionals who should be contacted

   Billing information and instructions

   Compensation for Healthcare Professional Executor

   Directions on how to disperse professional belongings

PROFESSIONAL WILL HANDOUT (P. 2)

5. Meet with an attorney specializing in health and mental health law to prepare the final Professional Will and keep on record.

6. Provide a copy of your Professional Will to your Healthcare Professional Executor and back-up designees.

7. Regularly review and update your Professional Will as needed.

8. Informed consent documentation provided to all clients should include the name of the Healthcare Professional Executor and their contact information.

Chapter 8

Ethics on a Cloudy Day

Developing Action Plans for Technologically Cloudy Questions

Objectives of Training

1. Develop an Ethical Action Plan to respond to technological ethical dilemmas

Description of Training

Ethics on a Cloudy Day: Developing Action Plans for Technologically Cloudy Questions brings ethics training into the modern era. Participants learn how to develop an Ethical Action Plan for responding to ethical dilemmas and "get their head out of the clouds." Ethical questions are presented reflecting new challenges and cloudy situations arising as a result of technological advances. This chapter is written in a manner that allows the trainer to keep up with modern technology by adding updated questions.

Intended Audience

Students, mental health professionals, other professionals, and organizations
Suitable for individuals, small, and large groups

Approximate Time Suggested for Training

1 hour

Materials suggested for training

Copy of an applicable Professional Code of Ethics for each participant
Paper and pen
Handouts

List of Handouts

Ethical Action Plan Handout
Ethical Action Plan Example #1 Handout
Ethical Action Plan Example #2 Handout
Ethical Use of Technology Questions Handout

Adaptations

To extend the length of this training, assign more questions to each group
To extend the length of this training, ask groups to develop their own questions related to technology and ethics
To stay abreast of technological advancements, the Ethical Use of Technology Questions Handout can be updated
Other professionals may substitute applicable questions

Procedures

1. Introductions, and review the objectives of the training. (5 minutes)
2. Distribute the Ethical Action Plan Handout to participants and review the steps to formulating an Ethical Action Plan. (5 minutes)
3. Distribute the Ethical Action Plan Example #1 and #2 Handouts to participants. Review each of the steps in the examples. (10 minutes)
4. Instruct participants to divide into small groups. Distribute to participants the Ethical Use of Technology Questions Handout. Assign one question to each group, so each group has a different dilemma. Instruct the groups to complete an Ethical Action Plan in writing. (15 minutes)
5. Ask each group to present their Ethical Action Plan to the group as a whole. (15 minutes)
6. Ask for final questions, comments, and closing statements. (5 minutes)

Bibliography

Devereaux, R. L., & Gottlieb, M. C. (2012). 'Record Keeping in the Cloud: Ethical Considerations.' *Professional Psychology: Research and Practice, 43,* 627–32

Fisher, C. B. (2017). *Decoding the Ethics Code: A Practical Guide for Psychologists, Fourth Edition.* Thousand Oaks, CA: Sage Publications, Inc.

Joint Task Force for the Development of Telepsychology Guidelines for Psychologists. (2013).
'Guidelines for the Practice of Telepsychology.' *American Psychologist, 68,* 791–800

Koocher, G. P., & Keith-Spiegel, P. (2016). *Ethics in Psychology and the Mental Health Professions: Standards and Cases, Fourth Edition.* Oxford, UK: Oxford University Press

Lannin, D. G., & Scott, N. A. (2013). 'Social Networking Ethics: Developing Best Practices for the New Small World.' *Professional Psychology: Research and Practice, 44,* 135–41

National Association of Social Work (N.A.S.W.). (2017). *Code of Ethics.* Retrieved from www.socialworkers.org/About/Ethics/Code-of-Ethics/Code-of-Ethics-English

Pope, K. S., & Vasquez, M. J. (2016). *Ethics in Psychotherapy and Counseling: A Practical Guide.* Hoboken, NJ: John Wiley & Sons, Inc.

Tribe, R., & Morrissey, J. (eds) (2015). *Handbook of Professional and Ethical Practice for Psychologists, Counsellors and Psychotherapists, Second Edition.* New York, NY: Routledge

Voshel, E. H., & Wesala, A. (2015). 'Social Media & Social Work Ethics: Determining Best Practices in an Ambiguous Reality.' *Journal of Social Work Values & Ethics, 12:1,* 67–76

Welfel, E. (2015). *Ethics in Counseling & Psychotherapy, Sixth Edition.* Boston MA: Cengage Learning

Zur Institute. *Telemental Health: The New Standard, Ethical, Legal, Clinical, Technological and Practice Considerations.* Retrieved from www.zurinstitute.com/telehealthcourse.html

HANDOUT 8.1: ETHICAL ACTION PLAN HANDOUT

What is my question?

Where can I get the information I need to answer this question?

By what specific date will I have this information?

What specific action(s) will I take once I have the required information?

By what specific date will I implement the action(s)?

When will I review this action plan for effectiveness?

HANDOUT 8.1A: ETHICAL ACTION PLAN EXAMPLE #1 HANDOUT

What is my question?

Does my professional liability insurance cover electronic communication in case of a complaint against me?

Where can I get the information I need to answer this question?

1. Read my professional liability insurance contract
2. Call my state licensing board to ask for recommended liability coverage
3. Call my professional liability insurance agent and get information on additional coverage

By what specific date will I have this information?

I will have the information by seven days from today (set the date).

What specific action(s) will I take once I have the required information?

1. If my professional liability insurance is adequate, there is no further action needed on my part
2. If my professional liability insurance does not adequately cover my electronic communication, I will choose a plan which will provide me with the coverage I want

By what specific date will I implement the action(s)?

I will have the coverage I want by 14 days from today (set the date)

When will I review this action plan for effectiveness?

Each year when I renew my professional liability insurance I will cross check my coverage with technological advances and the coverage recommended by my state licensing board.

HANDOUT 8.1B: ETHICAL ACTION PLAN EXAMPLE #2 HANDOUT

What is my question?

What should I do if my client posts a video of our therapy session online without my permission?

Where can I get the information I need to answer this question?

1. Check my Professional Code of Ethics for guidelines.
2. Ask my supervisor or consult with a colleague.
3. Call my state licensing board.
4. Consult with an attorney knowledgeable in mental health laws.

By what specific date will I have this information?

1. I will read my Code of Ethics today.
2. I will contact my supervisor or colleague today.
3. I will call my state licensing board today.
4. I will call an attorney for an immediate consult.

Due to the nature of the issue presented in this question, it is necessary to respond promptly.

What specific action(s) will I take once I have the required information?

I will decide on an action plan based on the information gathered and proceed accordingly. In this example, it might be necessary to develop further action plans based on the information gathered.

By what specific date will I implement the action(s)?

I will know what action to take by tomorrow.

When will I review this action plan for effectiveness?

I will review the action plan and the outcome with my supervisor or colleague in one week (set the date).

HANDOUT 8.2: USE OF ETHICAL TECHNOLOGY QUESTIONS HANDOUT

1. How can I ensure the confidentiality of clients on my phone contact list?
2. How do I verify client identity when using electronic communication?
3. How do I protect client confidentiality when using electronic communication?
4. What are the ethical guidelines to consider if a discharged client emails a request for clinical records?
5. What should I do if I breach confidential information while using electronic communication?
6. What safeguards can I put in place to guard against human error when using electronic communication?
7. Does my professional liability insurance cover electronic communication in case of a complaint against me?
8. What is the proper way to dispose of electronic devices with confidential information?
9. How can I assess client suitability and capacity for electronic and remote services?
10. Under what circumstances is it ethical for me to conduct an electronic search on a client?
11. What should I do if I know a colleague is breaching client confidentiality digitally?
12. What should I do if I know a colleague is using electronic communication with clients when under the influence of substances?
13. What cultural and socioeconomic factors should I consider when providing electronic services?
14. How can I ensure I am complying with all of the laws governing the use of technology?
15. How can I ensure I am competent to provide services using technology?
16. What should I do if a client posts a slanderous message about me online?
17. What should I do if my client posts online a video of our therapy session without my permission?
18. How do I ensure I am HIPPA compliant when audio or videotaping a session?
19. How do I define my digital boundaries?
20. In what ways are my digital boundaries different from my face-to-face boundaries?
21. What are potential risks for clients if I communicate with them digitally?

USE OF ETHICAL TECHNOLOGY QUESTIONS
HANDOUT (P. 2)

22. What are potential risks for me if I communicate with clients digitally after work hours?
23. What safeguards do I have in place to ensure I am keeping appropriate digital ethical boundaries?
24. Is it ethical for me to use client testimonials on my website?
25. What are the ethical guidelines to consider if I want to follow clients on social media?
26. What should I do if someone reveals they are my client on my social media site or blog?
27. How do I ensure emergency services if I provide services remotely?
28. What ethical guidelines should I consider if I am providing services to a client in a different time zone?
29. How do I delete digital files securely?
30. What do I have in place to ensure client confidentiality in the event of my incapacitation or death?

Chapter 9

Supervisory Ethics

Objectives of Training

1. Identify areas of growth needed to expand supervisory competence
2. Identify supervisory boundaries pertaining to technology
3. Describe recommended policies for remote and electronic supervision
4. Construct a Supervisory Genogram to explore diversity and multicultural issues

Description of Training

Supervisors will find 4 hours worth of training specifically designed to explore their ethical role and responsibilities in this chapter. Standards in Ethical Codes pertaining to supervision are reviewed with the participants. Written exercises and discussions are used to explore supervisory boundaries; remote and electronic supervision; evaluation of supervisees; and responses to ethical supervision dilemmas. Participants will also construct a Supervisory Genogram to explore their own supervision history.

Intended Audience

Students, mental health professionals, other professionals, and organizations
Suitable for individuals, small, and large groups

Approximate Time Suggested for Training

4 hours

Materials Suggested for Training

Copy of an applicable Professional Code of Ethics for each participant
White board or flip chart and markers
Paper and pens
Handouts

List of Handouts

Ethical Supervisory Competence Handout
Ethical Supervisory Boundary Handout
Ethical Supervisory Evaluation Handout
Ethical Supervisory Dilemmas Handout

Adaptations

This training can be shortened by limiting the handouts and questions
Other professionals may substitute applicable questions on the handouts

Procedures

1. Introductions, and review the objectives of the training. (10 minutes)

2. Distribute a copy of the applicable Professional Code of Ethics. Ask participants to highlight each Ethical Standard in their Professional Code of Ethics that pertains to providing supervision. Discuss the Ethical Standards which are identified. (15 minutes)

3. Explain that there will be silence as participants individually complete the Ethical Supervisory Competence Handout. Distribute the handout to participants and instruct them to write their answers to the questions on the form. Allow enough time for participants to complete the questions. The trainer can circulate around the room and provide support and guidance as needed. (20 minutes)

4. Instruct participants to find a partner with whom to share and discuss the Ethical Supervisory Competence Handout. (15 minutes)

5. Discuss with the large group any thoughts generated by the Ethical Supervisory Competence Handout. (10 minutes)

6. Explain that there will be silence as participants individually construct a Supervisory Genogram of the supervision they have received. Encourage them to include multicultural and diversity influences, therapeutic models, and the competencies of their own supervisors in this genogram. Ask for clarifying questions on the construction of a genogram before beginning. Allow enough time for participants to complete the genogram. The trainer can circulate around the room and provide support and guidance as needed. (15 minutes).

7. Instruct participants to find a partner with whom to share and discuss their Supervisory Genogram. (10 minutes)

8. Discuss with the large group any thoughts generated by the Supervisory Genograms, paying particular attention to any areas of growth or limitations identified. (10 minutes)

9. Explain that there will be silence as participants individually complete the Ethical Supervisory Boundary Handout. Distribute the handout to participants and instruct them to write their answers to the questions on the form. Allow enough time for participants to complete the questions. The trainer can circulate around the room and provide support and guidance as needed. (15 minutes)

10. Instruct participants to find a partner with whom to share and discuss the Ethical Supervisory Boundary Handout. (15 minutes)

11. Discuss with the large group any thoughts generated by the Ethical Supervisory Boundary Handout. (10 minutes)

12. Ask participants to highlight each Ethical Standard in their Professional Code of Ethics which pertains to providing remote and electronic

supervision. Discuss with the large group the benefits, limitations, and risks of providing remote and electronic supervision. (15 minutes)

13. Ask participants to list the guidelines and policies supervisors should have established prior to providing remote supervision. List these on the flip chart. (10 minutes)

14. Explain that there will be silence as participants individually complete the Ethical Supervisory Evaluation Handout. Distribute to participants the handout and instruct them to write their answers to the questions on the form. Allow enough time for them to complete the questions. The trainer can circulate around the room and provide support and guidance as needed. (15 minutes)

15. Instruct participants to find a partner with whom to share and discuss the Ethical Supervisory Evaluation Handout. (15 minutes)

16. Discuss with the large group any thoughts generated by the Ethical Supervisory Evaluation Handout. (15 minutes)

17. Distribute to participants the Ethical Supervisory Dilemmas Handout. Discuss each question as a large group and ask participants to identify applicable Ethical Standards from their Professional Code of Ethics. (20 minutes)

18. Ask for final questions, comments, and closing statements. (5 minutes)

Bibliography

American Association for Marriage and Family Therapy. (2015). *Code of Ethics (PDF File)*.Retrieved from www.aamft.org/iMIS15/AAMFT/Content/Legal_Ethics/Code_of_Ethics

American Counseling Association. (2014). *ACA Code of Ethics*. Retrieved from www.counseling.org/knowledge-center/ethics

American Mental Health Counselor Association. (2015). *Code of Ethics*. Retrieved from http://connections.amhca.org/viewdocument/amhca-code-of-ethics

American Psychological Association. (2017). *Ethical Principles of Psychologists and Code of Conduct*. Retrieved from www.apa.org/ethics/code/

Congress, E., Black, P., & Strom-Gottfried, K.(eds). (2009). *Teaching Social Work Values and Ethics: A Curriculum Resource*. Alexandria, VA: CSWE

Corey, G., Corey, M., & Corey, C. (2018). *Issues and Ethics in the Helping Professions, Tenth Edition*. Stamford, CT: Brooks/Cole Cengage Learning

Farber, B. A. (2006). *Self-Disclosure in Psychotherapy*. New York, NY: The Guilford Press

Fossen, C. M., Anderson-Meger, J. I., & Daehn Zellmer, D. A. (2014). 'Infusing a New Ethical Decision Making Model Throughout a BSW Curriculum.' *Journal of Social Work Values and Ethics, 11:1,* 66–81

Koocher, G. P., & Keith-Spiegel, P. (2016). *Ethics in Psychology and the Mental Health Professions: Standards and Cases, Fourth Edition*. Oxford, UK: Oxford University Press

Levitt, D. H., & Moorhead, H. J. H. (eds) (2013). *Values & Ethics in Counseling: Real-Life Decision Making*. New York, NY: Routledge

National Association of Social Work (N.A.S.W.). (2017). *Code of Ethics*. Retrieved from www.socialworkers.org/About/Ethics/Code-of-Ethics/Code-of-Ethics-English

National Board for Certified Counselors (NBCC). (2013). *Code of Ethics*. Retrieved from www.nbcc.org/Ethics/CodeOfEthics

Pope, K. S., & Vasquez, M. J. (2016). *Ethics in Psychotherapy and Counseling: A Practical Guide*. Hoboken, NJ: John Wiley & Sons, Inc.

Thomas, J. T. (2010). *The Ethics of Supervision and Consultation: Practical Guidelines for Mental Health Professionals*. Washington, D.C.: American Psychological Association

Tribe, R., & Morrissey, J. (eds) (2015). *Handbook of Professional and Ethical Practice for Psychologists, Counsellors and Psychotherapists, Second Edition*. New York, NY: Routledge

Voshel, E. H., & Wesala, A. (2015). 'Social Media & Social Work Ethics: Determining Best Practices in an Ambiguous Reality.' *Journal of Social Work Values & Ethics, 12:1,* 67–76

Welfel, E. (2015). *Ethics in Counseling & Psychotherapy, Sixth Edition*. Boston, MA: Cengage Learning

HANDOUT 9.1: ETHICAL SUPERVISORY COMPETENCE HANDOUT

1. Identify the training you have received to provide supervision.

2. Identify the training you have received in diversity and multicultural awareness.

3. What model of supervision do you follow?

4. How does your supervision style change with the developmental needs of the supervisee?

5. Identify area(s) of clinical competence which you are qualified to supervise.

6. Identify the limitation(s) in your clinical competence pertaining to supervision.

7. Identify your desired area(s) of growth relating to your competence in supervision.

HANDOUT 9.2: ETHICAL SUPERVISORY BOUNDARY HANDOUT

1. What boundaries do you establish with your supervisees?

2. What technological boundaries do you establish with your supervisees?

3. During which specific hours do you respond to:
   - phone calls from supervisees?
   - emails from supervisees?
   - texts from supervisees?

4. How do you ensure your supervisees are maintaining appropriate boundaries with their own clients?

5. How many supervisees are you willing to supervise at any one point in time?

6. What are your boundaries of self-disclosure to supervisees?

HANDOUT 9.3: ETHICAL SUPERVISORY EVALUATION HANDOUT

1. What procedure(s) do you follow when evaluating your supervisees?

2. How do you evaluate the emotional competency of your supervisees?

3. How do you evaluate if your supervisees can contain and tolerate clinical material?

4. What informal practice(s) do you have in place to receive feedback from your supervisees?

5. What formal practice(s) do you have in place to receive feedback from your supervisees?

HANDOUT 9.4: ETHICAL SUPERVISORY DILEMMAS HANDOUT

1. A supervisee offers you their vacation home free of charge for one week. What is your response?

2. Your supervisee introduces you to a client as their friend. What is your response?

3. Your organization has hired a former client and assigned you as their supervisor. What is your response?

4. Your supervisee invites you to a dinner party at his/her home. What is your response?

5. A supervisee comes to supervision appearing disheveled and unkempt. What is your response?

6. You find the pictures on your supervisee's office walls offensive. What is your response?

7. A supervisee has falsified client documentation. What is your response?

8. A supervisee has repeatedly falsified client documentation. What is your response?

9. Your supervisee is politically outspoken and has a visible presence in the community. You have growing concerns that their political views are resulting in prejudices and biases in their clinical work. What is your response?

Chapter 10

Developing Ethical Resources

Objectives of Training

1. Identify resources for ethical practice
2. Design an Ethical Resource Action Plan

Description of Training

Many trauma-informed therapies include the development of resources for clients as an initial step in the treatment process. Using this as a model, participants are led through an exercise to identify resources for ethical practice. Participants will then choose one ethical resource and design an Ethical Resource Action Plan to ensure its implementation.

Intended Audience

Students, mental health professionals, other professionals, and organizations
Suitable for individuals, small, and large groups

Approximate Time Suggested for Training

1 hour

Materials Suggested for Training

Paper and pens (participants are encouraged to bring their own journals)
Handouts

List of Handouts

Ethical Resource Questionnaire Handout
Ethical Resource Action Plan Handout

Adaptations

Professionals may substitute appropriate wording on the Ethical Resource Questionnaire Handout and Ethical Resource Action Plan Handout
For clients, modify handouts to fit client specific issues

Procedures

1. Introductions, and review the objectives of the training. (5 minutes)
2. Distribute the Ethical Resource Questionnaire Handout. Explain that the questions can be answered on the handout or in their journals. (20 minutes)
3. Briefly discuss the process of completing the resource questionnaire with participants. Ask what they learned from the experience. (10 minutes)
4. Distribute the Ethical Resource Action Plan Handout. Explain that the questions can be answered on the handout or in their journals. (10 minutes)
5. Ask each participant to find a partner and present their action plan to one another. (10)
6. Ask for final questions, comments, and closing statements. (5 minutes)

Bibliography

Corey, G., Corey, M., & Corey, C. (2018). *Issues and Ethics in the Helping Professions, Tenth Edition*. Stamford, CT: Brooks/Cole Cengage Learning

Joint Task Force for the Development of Telepsychology Guidelines for Psychologists. (2013).

'Guidelines for the Practice of Telepsychology'. *American Psychologist, 68,* 791–800

Koocher, G. P., & Keith-Spiegel, P. (2016). *Ethics in Psychology and the Mental Health Professions: Standards and Cases, Fourth Edition*. Oxford, UK: Oxford University Press

Knapp, S. J., Gottleib, M. C., Handlesman, M. M., & VandeCreek, L. D., (eds). (2012) *APA Handbook of Ethics in Psychology*. Washington, D.C.: American Psychological Association

Lannin, D. G., & Scott, N. A. (2013). 'Social Networking Ethics: Developing Best Practices for the New Small World.' *Professional Psychology: Research and Practice, 44,* 135–41

Miller-Karas, E. (2015). *Building Resilience to Trauma: The Trauma and Community Resilience Models*. New York, NY: Routledge

Ogden, P., & Fisher, J. (2015). *Sensorimotor Psychotherapy: Interventions for Trauma and Attachment*. New York, NY: Norton Books

Pope, K. S., & Vasquez, M. J. (2016). *Ethics in Psychotherapy and Counseling: A Practical Guide*. Hoboken, NJ: John Wiley & Sons, Inc.

Reamer, F. G. (2001). *The Social Work Ethics Audit: A Risk Management Tool*. Washington, D.C.: N.A.S.W. Press

Strom-Gottfried, K. (2016). *Straight Talk About Professional Ethics, Second Edition*. Oxford, UK: Oxford University Press

Tribe, R., & Morrissey, J. (eds) (2015). *Handbook of Professional and Ethical Practice for Psychologists, Counsellors and Psychotherapists, Second Edition*. New York, NY: Routledge

HANDOUT 10.1: ETHICAL RESOURCE QUESTIONNAIRE HANDOUT

1. What written materials on ethics do you have in your professional library?

2. What online ethical resources do you regularly consult?

3. Who are the specific supervisors and consultants you trust for ethical guidance?

4. Which colleagues do you trust for ethical guidance?

5. What are your specific symptoms of overload, hopelessness, and burn-out?

6. What self-care practices do you need to maintain a healthy professional life?

7. How do you gain and maintain competence in work with diverse populations?

8. How can you stay abreast of changes in technology which impact your service?

9. How can you stay abreast of new techniques and evidence-based practices?

10. How do you ensure the obtainment of a wide variety of training?

11. What are your areas of competence?

12. What are the limitations in your practice?

13. How do you maintain your areas of competence?

14. How do you ensure your limitations do not become ethical liabilities?

15. What professional supports do you have in place?

16. How do you ensure competence in the professionals to whom you refer others?

17. What physical, emotional, and creative outlets do you have outside of work?

18. What risk management or auditing practices do you have in place for your practice?

HANDOUT 10.2: ETHICAL RESOURCE ACTION PLAN HANDOUT

1. What resources do you notice are lacking in your professional practice?

2. Choose one resource which you are lacking and write a plan of action on how to develop this resource.

3. What is your timeline to carry out this plan of action?

4. How will you hold yourself accountable for this plan of action?

Chapter 11

Developing Ethical Rituals

Objectives of Training

1. Discuss how rituals in relate to ethical efficacy professional practice

Description of Training

Developing Ethical Rituals engages helping professionals in a combination of contemplative exercises with expressive arts to explore the meaning they ascribe to ethics. Participants study their applicable Professional Code of Ethics and choose an object to symbolize an Ethical Value, Ethical Principle, or Ethical Standard (such as a box to symbolize a boundary). They are guided through a journaling exercise, which leads them to identify and adopt new ethical rituals in their practice.

Intended Audience

Students, mental health professionals, other professionals, clients, and organizations
Suitable for individuals, small, and large groups

Approximate Time Suggested for Training

1 hour

Materials Suggested for Training

Copy of an applicable Professional Code of Ethics for each participant

An assortment of objects from nature, sand tray miniatures, jewelry, ornaments, and small items displayed on a table (participants are encouraged to bring one object of their own choosing)

Paper and pens (participants are encouraged to bring their own journals)

White board or flip chart and markers

Handout

List of Handouts

Ethical Rituals Handout

Adaptations

Other professionals may substitute an applicable Professional Code of Ethics

For clients substitute the word "morals" for "ethics"

Organizations may substitute the organization as a whole for the individual practice of the professional

Procedures

1. Introductions, and review the objectives of the training. (5 minutes)
2. Distribute a copy of the applicable Professional Code of Ethics to each participant. Ask them to look it over, notice what catches their attention, and highlight those words or sections. (5 minutes)
3. Participants are instructed to look at the items displayed on the table and choose one which represents an Ethical Core Value, Ethical Principle, or Ethical Standard (such as a box to symbolize a boundary) from their Professional Code of Ethics. Other options include having participants bring their own object to the training or to quickly go outside and find a small object in nature to bring inside. (5 minutes)
4. Instruct participants to place the object in front of them. Distribute the Ethical Rituals Handout and ask them to write their answers on the handout or in their journal. (15 minutes)
5. Ask participants if anyone wants to share briefly their experience with this exercise and what they have learned from it. (10 minutes)
6. Ask participants to list current intentional rituals integrated into their professional practice and write these on the white board. (5 minutes)
7. Instruct participants to write down two more rituals on their handout or in their journals that they want to add to their professional practice to cultivate ethical efficacy. (5 minutes)
8. Ask participants to find a partner and share the two rituals that they want to add to their professional practice. (5 minutes)
9. Ask for final questions, comments, and closing statements. (5 minutes)

Bibliography

Abels, S. (2001). *Ethics in Social Work Practice: Narratives for Professional Helping.* Denver, CO: Love Publishing

American Association for Marriage and Family Therapy. (2015). *Code of Ethics* (PDF File). Retrieved from www.aamft.org/iMIS15/AAMFT/Content/Legal_Ethics/Code_of_Ethics

American Counseling Association. (2014). *ACA Code of Ethics.* Retrieved from www.counseling.org/knowledge-center/ethics

American Mental Health Counselor Association. (2015). *Code of Ethics.* Retrieved from http://connections.amhca.org/viewdocument/amhca-code-of-ethics

American Psychological Association. (2017). *Ethical Principles of Psychologists and Code of Conduct.* Retrieved from www.apa.org/ethics/code/

Atkins, S. & Snyder, M. (2018). *Nature-Based Expressive Art Therapy: Integrating the Expressive Arts and Ecotherapy.* Philadelphia, PA: Jessica Kingsley Publishers

National Association of Social Work (N.A.S.W.). (2017). *Code of Ethics.* Retrieved from www.socialworkers.org/About/Ethics/Code-of-Ethics/Code-of-Ethics-English

National Board for Certified Counselors (N.B.C.C.). (2013). *Code of Ethics.* Retrieved from www.nbcc.org/Ethics/CodeOfEthics

HANDOUT 11.1: ETHICAL RITUALS HANDOUT

1. What is the symbolic meaning(s) of your object?

2. How does it relate specifically to ethical practice and decision making?

3. What are some multicultural implications of this object?

4. Referring to your Professional Code of Ethics, list specific Core Ethical Values, Ethical Principles, or Ethical Standards that your object represents.

5. How can you integrate this object into your practice by using it to create a ritual?

6. What intentional rituals do you already have in your practice?

Section Three

Using Expressive Arts to Learn Ethics

Section Summary: Using Expressive Arts to Learn Ethics

Participants have described the trainings in this section as innovative, enjoyable, refreshing, energizing, provocative, and stimulating. Expressive arts involve the use of movement, mind-body connection, art materials, modeling clay, and mask making. Learning is accomplished in this section, entitled *Using Expressive Arts to Learn Ethics*, through all three learning styles: auditory, visual, and kinesthetic.

Expressive arts help participants to understand and internalize ethics through experience in the body. This integration leads to a deeper appreciation, and accessibility to an ideal ethical identity.

Chapter 12

Setting Ethical Boundaries With Your Body gives participants an alternative way of thinking about boundaries. It gets participants up, moving, and thinking about the relationship between the mind-body connection and ethical decision making. It is easy to adapt this training for work with clients.

Chapter 13

Embodied Ethics offers an opportunity to understand how attuning to one's body aids in making sound ethical decisions. This training combines expressive arts with contemplative exercises in a unique way to identify Ethical Core Values and Ethical Principles. It is also a powerful exercise with some simple adaptations for work with clients.

Chapter 14

Ethics in Motion combines using body and sensory awareness as an effective means of understanding ethics and technology. It includes using a game of Password, which further engages participants in their learning process. With minor adaptations this training is valuable for teaching clients and client groups how feelings and emotions are expressed through their body.

Chapter 15

The Many Faces of Ethics: Making Masks uses art making, guided imagery, written exercises, and discussion to learn ethics in a novel way. Helping professionals as well as clients can benefit from this training which explores the internal and external images we present to the world.

Chapter 16

The Grain of Truth: Enacting Ethics Through the Use of Sand Trays builds upon the exploration of multiple relationships, diversity, and boundaries within the context of group and individual activities. Sand trays are used throughout the training as symbolic representations of ethical issues and an ethical identity. A guided imagery and written exercises guide participants in resolving an ethical dilemma.

Chapter 17

Ethical Sculptures incorporates the use of modeling clay and an interactive family sculpting exercise. A written exercise allows for contemplation and an opportunity for discussion. This training actively engages participants in auditory, visual, and kinesthetic learning.

Chapter 18

Creating Ethical Super Powers is a lighthearted way to teach the serious subject of the potential for ethical misuse or abuse in the power dynamic between professional and client. Quick sketches are made to facilitate ethical awareness and discussion.

Chapter 12

Setting Ethical Boundaries with Your Body

Objectives of Training

1. Define boundaries and terms related to boundaries
2. Recognize the relationship between the mind-body connection and ethical decision making

Description of Training

Setting Ethical Boundaries With Your Body is an ideal opportunity for helping professionals to somatically explore this prevalent topic of ethics. Participants discuss the definition of boundaries and terms related to boundaries. Various types of somatic boundaries are then reviewed and participants are asked to explore these boundaries with physical poses. They are led through an exercise recalling recent ethical decisions and identifying the mind-body connection to these decisions. This quick, one-hour training is excellent for both new and experienced helping professionals alike.

Intended Audience

Students, mental health professionals, other professionals, clients, and organizations
Suitable for individuals, small, and large groups

Approximate Time Suggested for Training

1 hour

Materials Suggested for Training

Whiteboard or flip chart and markers
Handouts

List of Handouts

Boundary Terms

Adaptations

For clients, substitute personal decisions for ethical decisions

Procedures

1. Introductions, and review the objectives of the training. (5 minutes)
2. Ask the participants to define the following terms and write them on the white board (the trainer can refer to the Boundary Terms Handout). Ask for examples of each term. Depending on the size of the group, participants could be divided into smaller groups and then report back to the group as a whole. (15 minutes)
   - Boundaries
   - Boundary issues
   - Boundary crossings and extensions
   - Boundary violation
   - Somatic boundary
3. Ask the participants to list examples of somatic boundaries on the white board. (5 minutes)
4. Instruct the participants to stand up with space around them to move. Explain that you will read the words from the list of examples of somatic boundaries one at a time and the participants will assume a physical pose, facial expression, or movement which depicts the somatic boundary. Read the list slowly to allow the participants time to fully move into different poses, expressions, or movements. (10 minutes)
5. Instruct the participants to be seated and lead a discussion to process what they learned from the experience. (5 minutes)
6. Instruct the participants to find a partner and sit facing one another. Explain they will choose one person to go first. The trainer will read the following instructions very slowly. (5 minutes)
   - *Think of a wise ethical decision you have made in the last week*
     - *Verbally tell your partner*
     - *Take a deep breath*
     - *Tell your partner what you notice in your body when thinking of a wise ethical decision*
     - *Identify where in your body you feel wise decisions lie*
   - *Think of an unwise ethical decision you or someone you have heard of has made*
     - *Tell your partner*
     - *Take a breath*
     - *Tell your partner what you notice in your body when thinking of an unwise ethical decision*
     - *Identify where in your body you feel unwise decisions lie*
7. Instruct the participants to switch roles and repeat the above exercise. (5 minutes)
8. Instruct the participants to be seated and lead a discussion to process what they learned from the experience. (5 minutes)
9. Ask for final questions, comments, and closing statements. (5 minutes)

Bibliography

Damasio, A. R. (2000). *The Feeling of What Happens: Body and Emotion in the Making of Consciousness.* Orlando, FL: Harcourt Books

Fogel, A. (2009). *Body Sense: The Science and Practice of Embodied Self-Awareness.* New York, NY: W. W. Norton

Levine, P. A. (2010). *In an Unspoken Voice: How the Body Releases Trauma and Restores Greatness.* Berkeley, CA: North Atlantic Books

Miller-Karas, E. (2015). *Building Resilience to Trauma: The Trauma and Community Resilience Models.* New York, NY: Routledge

Ogden, P., & Fisher, J. (2015). *Sensorimotor Psychotherapy: Interventions for Trauma and Attachment.* New York, NY: Norton Books

Ogden, P., Minton, K., & Pain, C. (2006). *Trauma and the Body: A Sensorimotor Approach to Psychotherapy.* New York, NY: Norton

Painter, C. V. (2017). *The Wisdom of the Body: A Contemplative Journey to Wholeness for Women.* Notre Dame, IN: Sorin Books

Reamer, F. G. (2012). *Boundary Issues and Dual Relationships in the Human Services.* New York, NY: Columbia University Press

Strom-Gottfried, K. (2016). *Straight Talk About Professional Ethics, Second Edition.* Oxford, UK: Oxford University Press

Van Der Kolk, Bessel, M. D. (2014). *The Body Keeps the Score.* New York, NY: Viking

Welfel, E. R. (2016). *Ethics in Counseling and Psychotherapy: Standards, Research and Emerging Issues, Sixth Edition.* Boston, MA: Cengage Learning

Zur, O. (2007). *Boundaries in Psychotherapy: Ethical and Clinical Explorations.* Washington, DC: American Psychological Association

HANDOUT 12.1: BOUNDARY TERMS

Boundaries – defines an area around a person or a limit of ethical behavior

Boundary issues – a breach of agreement by one or both parties

Boundary crossings and extensions – the beginning of a breach, which is not harmful and does not exploit the client

Boundary violation – a breach that exploits a client

Somatic boundary – personal body space

Chapter 13

Embodied Ethics

Objectives of Training

1. Explain the differences between Professional Qualities, Ethical Core Values, and Ethical Principles
2. Identify and attune to where in the body Professional Qualities, Ethical Core Values, and Ethical Principles are located

Description of Training

Embodied Ethics is an innovative method of contemplating and experiencing ethics drawing upon current research on the wisdom of our bodies. This expressive arts activity is designed to assist participants in understanding how the role of attuning to one's body aids in making sound ethical decisions.

Intended Audience

Students, mental health professionals, other professionals, clients, and organizations
Suitable for individuals, small, and large groups

Approximate Time Suggested for Training

2 hours

Materials Suggested for Training

Paper, pen or pencil
One piece of card stock for human figure (handout)
Scissors
Three-quarter-inch round color-coding adhesive labels in two colors (four labels in each color per participant)
Whiteboard and markers
Copy of an applicable Professional Code of Ethics for each participant
Handouts

List of Handouts

List of Ethical Core Values and Ethical Principles Handout
Professional Qualities and Ethical Core Values and Ethical Principles Handout
Human Figure Handout

Adaptations

Other professionals may substitute applicable professional Ethical Values
For clients substitute personal values for the Ethical Values
Organizations may substitute organizational values for Ethical Values

Procedures

1. Introductions, and review the objectives of the training. (10 minutes)
2. Explain the concept of Professional Qualities as personality traits, attributes, characteristics, and skills. Ask participants to give examples of Professional Qualities and write these on the whiteboard. (5 minutes)
3. Explain the concept of Ethical Core Values, which are the fundamental beliefs and guiding principles forming the foundation for actions. Ask participants to name a few and write these on the whiteboard. (5 minutes)
4. Explain the concept of Ethical Principles, which are Ethical Standards, moral codes, creeds, and laws. Ask participants to give examples of Ethical Principles and write these on the whiteboard. (5 minutes)
5. Explain that each professional discipline has a Professional Code of Ethics, which set Ethical Standards and expectations of conduct and decision-making based on Ethical Values and Ethical Principles. Ask for questions and comments before proceeding. (5 minutes)
6. Distribute the Professional Qualities, Ethical Core Values and Ethical Principles Handout.
7. Explain that the next series of instructions will be completed with no talking in the group. Instruct participants to write a list of four Professional Qualities that they bring to their professional practice on the left-hand side of the handout. (10 minutes)
8. Distribute the List of Ethical Core Values and Ethical Principles Handout and the Professional Code of Ethics applicable to their professional discipline. Instruct participants to write a list of four Ethical Core Values and Ethical Principles that they bring to their professional practice on the right hand side of the first handout. (15 minutes)
9. Distribute four of the three-quarter-inch round color-coding adhesive labels in two colors (four of each color). Instruct participants to write each of their listed Professional Qualities on four labels of one color. (5 minutes)
10. Instruct participants to write out each of their Ethical Core Values and Ethical Principles on four labels of the second color. (5 minutes)
11. Instruct participants to draw a human figure on the piece of card stock paper which they may cut out if so desired. Alternatively the human figure in the handouts can be used. (5 minutes)
12. Read the following out loud:
    Place the human figure in front of you. As you pick up each of the labels, if your are comfortable close your eyes, take three deep breaths. While you are breathing deeply think of the word(s) written on your label and locate where on/in your body you feel or associate it (embodiment).

Open your eyes and attach the label on your human figure. Repeat this with each label. Take as much time as you need as you attune to your body with each Professional Quality and Ethical Principle. (15 minutes)

13. When all participants have completed attaching the labels to the human figure, read out loud the following:

    When you have attuned to each Professional Quality, Ethical Core Value, and Ethical Principle in your body, and all the labels are attached to the human figure, step back from it and explore it deeply. Identify if any sensations are present. Attune to your full body. Then take a moment to write down any observations you have made. (5 minutes)

14. Discuss as a group the following questions: (25 minutes)

    - Are you balanced in your body with the Professional Qualities and Ethical Principles?
    - Are all three intelligence centers represented in your human figure (thinking mind, feeling heart, and instinctual intuition)?
    - Notice what you might want to pay attention to in the future.
    - Do you want something to change professionally?
    - How can you use this experience in your clinical practice?

15. Ask for final questions, comments, and closing statements. (5 minutes)

Bibliography

American Association for Marriage and Family Therapy. (2015). *Code of Ethics (PDF File)*.Retrieved from www.aamft.org/iMIS15/AAMFT/Content/Legal_Ethics/Code_of_Ethics

American Counseling Association. (2014). *ACA Code of Ethics*. Retrieved from www.counseling.org/knowledge-center/ethics

American Mental Health Counselor Association. (2015). *Code of Ethics*. Retrieved from http://connections.amhca.org/viewdocument/amhca-code-of-ethics

American Psychological Association. (2017). *Ethical Principles of Psychologists and Code of Conduct*. Retrieved from www.apa.org/ethics/code/

Damasio, A. R. (2000). *The Feeling of What Happens: Body and Emotion in the Making of Consciousness*. Orlando, FL: Harcourt Books

Fogel, A. (2009). *Body Sense: The Science and Practice of Embodied Self-Awareness*. New York, NY: W. W. Norton

Koocher, G. P., & Keith-Spiegel, P. (2016). *Ethics in Psychology & the Mental Health Professions: Standards and Cases, Fourth Edition*. Oxford, UK: Oxford University Press

Levine, P. A. (2010). *In an Unspoken Voice: How the Body Releases Trauma and Restores Greatness*. Berkeley, CA: North Atlantic Books

Miller-Karas, E. (2015). *Building Resilience to Trauma: The Trauma and Community Resilience Models*. New York, NY: Routledge

National Association of Social Work (N.A.S.W.). (2017). *Code of Ethics*. Retrieved from www.socialworkers.org/About/Ethics/Code-of-Ethics/Code-of-Ethics-English

National Board for Certified Counselors (N.B.C.C.). (2013). *Code of Ethics*. Retrieved from www.nbcc.org/Ethics/CodeOfEthics

Ogden, P., & Fisher, J. (2015). *Sensorimotor Psychotherapy: Interventions for Trauma and Attachment*. New York, NY: Norton Books

Ogden, P., Minton, K., & Pain, C. (2006). *Trauma and the Body: A Sensorimotor Approach to Psychotherapy*. New York, NY: Norton

Painter, C. V. (2017). *The Wisdom of the Body: A Contemplative Journey to Wholeness for Women*. Notre Dame, IN: Sorin Books

Sandmaier, M. (2017). 'Doorways to the Embodied Self: Eugene Gendlin and the Felt Sense.' *Psychotherapy Networker, 41: 4*, 39–46

Van Der Kolk, Bessel, M. D. (2014). *The Body Keeps the Score*. New York, NY: Viking

Welfel, E. R. (2016). *Ethics in Counseling and Psychotherapy: Standards, Research, and Emerging Issues, Sixth Edition*. Boston, MA: Centage Learning

HANDOUT 13.1: LIST OF ETHICAL CORE VALUES AND ETHICAL PRINCIPLES HANDOUT

Autonomy

Beneficence

Competence

Confidentiality

Dignity and worth of the person

Education and training standards

Fidelity

Honoring diversity

Importance of human relationships

Integrity

Non-maleficence

Remuneration

Research standards

Service

Social justice

Supervisor responsibility

Veracity

HANDOUT 13.1A: PROFESSIONAL QUALITIES AND ETHICAL CORE VALUES AND ETHICAL PRINCIPLES HANDOUT

Professional Qualities	Ethical Core Values and Ethical Principles

HANDOUT 13.2: HUMAN FIGURE

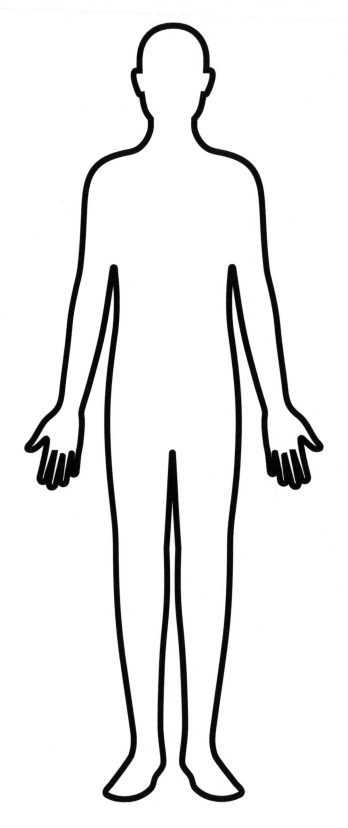

Chapter 14

Ethics in Motion

Objectives of Training

1. Identify body sensations and awareness when faced with ethical dilemmas related to technology

Description of Training

This innovative training exercise, *Ethics in Motion*, combines learning ethics through body and sensory awareness with addressing modern issues related to technology. Participants are led through an activity involving making gestures representing a variety of feelings and emotions, such as self-confidence, shame, and fear. The trainer facilitates a discussion of the relation of these gestures to ethical challenges. Using the Gendlin Method of Focusing, participants will identify body sensations and awareness as specific Ethical Case Dilemmas are presented. These cases are then discussed by referring to applicable Professional Ethical Codes. The final activity includes a game of team Password, using sensory vocabulary (adapted from Ogden's Sensorimotor Psychotherapy) and answering questions of ethical dilemmas related to technology.

Intended Audience

Students, mental health professionals, other professionals, clients, and organizations
Suitable for small and large groups

Approximate Time Suggested for Training

3 hours

Materials Suggested for Training

Copy of an applicable Professional Code of Ethics for each participant
Printed Sensory Words Related to Ethics Handout (with the words cut out)
Printed Ethical Questions Related to Technology Handout (with the words cut out)
Two bowls (for the password clues and ethical questions)
Large whiteboard or flip chart and markers
Timer
Handouts

List of Handouts

Sensory Words Related to Ethics Handout
Ethical Questions Related to Technology Handout

Adaptations

To shorten the length of the training, limit the activities presented
Large groups will require additional trainers to conduct the Password game
Other professionals may substitute applicable professional ethical questions
For clients, substitute situational questions for the ethical questions
Organizations may substitute situational questions for the ethical questions

Procedures

1. Introductions, and review the objectives of the training. (10 minutes)
2. Explain that the following exercise is adapted from *Building Resilience to Trauma* and will involve participants making gestures from a standing position.
3. Ask participants to stand up and allow for space to move about freely. The trainer will read the following instructions very slowly to give adequate time for thoughtful movement and gestures. (10 minutes)
   - *Think of a gesture which represents self-soothing... then make the gesture. As you are making the gesture, notice what is happening inside your body.*
   - *Think of a gesture which represents self-confidence...then make the gesture. As you are making the gesture, notice what is happening inside your body.*
   - *Think of a gesture which represents joy...then make the gesture. As you are making the gesture, notice what is happening inside your body.*
   - *Think of a gesture which represents disgust...then make the gesture. As you are making the gesture, notice what is happening inside your body.*
   - *Think of a gesture which represents surprise...then make the gesture. As you are making the gesture, notice what is happening inside your body.*
   - *Think of a gesture which represents shame...then make the gesture. As you are making the gesture, notice what is happening inside your body.*
   - *Think of a gesture which represents fear...then make the gesture. As you are making the gesture, notice what is happening inside your body.*
   - *Think of a gesture which represents pride...then make the gesture. As you are making the gesture, notice what is happening inside your body.*
4. While the participants are standing, ask them to discuss the following questions (participants may choose to sit down after the first question is answered). (15 minutes)
   - *Describe this experience.*
   - *Did you notice any patterns?*
   - *Do you have any new understanding of how your body and mind connect?*
   - *How does this exercise relate to ethics and ethical decision making?*

5. Tell participants they can choose to remain standing, sit or lie on the floor, or sit in their chairs for the next series of instructions, which are adapted from Eugene Gendlin's work on Focusing. The trainer will read the following instructions very slowly. (10 minutes)
   - *Close your eyes and quiet yourself.*
   - *Focus on the sensations in your body.*
   - *Now try to find a word, phrase, or image that matches the sensation you feel in your body.*
   - *Does this sensation have anything to tell you?*
   - *What does it want you to know?*
   - *Focus on a body part (stomach, eyes, feet) and I'll tell you a word - keep returning to the focus of this body part.*
   - *Respectable*
   - *Fearful (remember to return to your focused body part)*
   - *Assured*
   - *Irritable (remember to return to your focused body part)*
   - *Triggered*
   - *Composed (remember to return to your focused body part)*

6. Request that participants return to their seats. Ask them to discuss what they noticed during the exercise. (5 minutes)

7. Ask the participants into which therapeutic modalities Gendlin's Focusing has been integrated? (Somatic Experiencing, I.F.S., E.M.D.R., Sensorimotor Psychotherapy, Guided Imagery, energy therapies are some possibilities.) (5 minutes)

8. Instruct the participants to position themselves in their chairs in a manner that represents taking an ethical stance.

9. Now instruct the participants to position themselves in their chairs in a manner that represents an unethical stance.

10. Ask the participants to discuss in small groups the correlation between Focusing and ethical decision making. (15 minutes)

11. Ask if any of the groups want to report back to the large group particulars from their discussion. (5 minutes)

12. Instruct each of the small groups to develop a brief Ethical Case Dilemma (1 to 3 sentences) and have them write it down and turn it in to you. (15 minutes)

13. Read out the brief Ethical Case Dilemmas written by the groups and ask the participants to pay attention to their bodies. While reading out the brief dilemmas, alternate instructions so participants go back and forth between positioning themselves in their chairs taking an ethical stance, and then taking an unethical stance. Ask for comments and discussion after each dilemma is read. (15 minutes)

14. Divide the participants into two teams (A and B, or teams can come up with their own name). Have them move their chairs so each team is grouped together and faces the front of the room. (5 minutes)

15. Explain the rules to Team Password:
    Both teams choose one team member to come up to the front of the room (this person is called the Clue Giver). The trainer chooses one Clue Giver to start (Team A). The Clue Giver picks one piece of paper from the Password Bowl provided by the trainer and looks at it without talking. The Clue Giver has 1 minute (trainer sets a timer) to think of a one-word clue. Clues cannot use any configuration of the password and must only be one word. When the timer goes off, Team A's Clue Giver presents a one-word clue to their team. Team A discusses it out loud and must agree on the answer in 2 minutes and announce it (trainer sets the timer). If they get it right, Team A scores ten points (trainer records the points on the whiteboard or flip chart). If they get it wrong, Team B's Clue Giver looks at the password and has 1 minute (set timer) to give a one-word clue to their team. If Team B answers correctly in 1 minute (set timer), they earn nine points. This goes back and forth, with the password value continuing to decrease, until 1) the word is guessed; 2) ten clues are given without a correct guess; or 3) the password is said by a Clue Giver, in which case the word is thrown out. If the word is not guessed after ten clues, then the Clue Givers can tell both teams the password.

16. Explain that each team has an opportunity to earn another ten points by answering an ethics question related to technology. Team B's Clue Giver picks out one piece of paper from the Ethics Questions Bowl and reads it out loud to both teams. The two clue givers rejoin their teams to discuss and agree upon an answer. The trainer sets a timer for 3 minutes and asks for each team's answer when the timer goes off. The trainer has the authority to decide whether the team's answer earns ten points and records the points on the whiteboard or flip chart.

17. Explain that each team has an opportunity to earn another five points by relating the password to the ethics question. The trainer sets a timer for 1 minute while the two teams decide upon an answer. The trainer has the authority to decide whether each team's answer earns five points and records the points.

18. The game continues on until all the passwords and ethical questions have been processed. For each complete round of passwords and questions new Clue Givers are chosen. (60 minutes)

19. Ask for final questions, comments, and closing statements.

Bibliography

Damasio, A. R. (2000). *The Feeling of What Happens: Body and Emotion in the Making of Consciousness*. Orlando, FL: Harcourt Books

Gendlin, E. (1996). *Focusing-Oriented Psychotherapy: A Manual of the Experiential Method*. New York, NY: The Guilford Press

Fogel, A. (2009). *Body Sense: The Science and Practice of Embodied Self-Awareness*. New York, NY: W. W. Norton

Koocher, G. P., & Keith-Spiegel, P. (2016). *Ethics in Psychology and the Mental Health Professions: Standards and Cases, Fourth Edition*. Oxford, UK: Oxford University Press

Levine, P. A. (2010). *In an Unspoken Voice: How the Body Releases Trauma and Restores Greatness*. Berkeley, CA: North Atlantic Books

Miller-Karas, E. (2015). *Building Resilience to Trauma: The Trauma and Community Resilience Models*. New York, NY: Routledge

Ogden, P., & Fisher, J. (2015). *Sensorimotor Psychotherapy: Interventions for Trauma and Attachment*. New York, NY: Norton Books

Ogden, P., Minton, K., & Pain, C. (2006). *Trauma and the Body: A Sensorimotor Approach to Psychotherapy*. New York, NY: Norton

Painter, C. V. (2017). *The Wisdom of the Body: A Contemplative Journey to Wholeness for Women*. Notre Dame, IN: Sorin Books

Pope, K. S., & Vasquez, M. J. (2016). *Ethics in Psychotherapy and Counseling: A Practical Guide*. Hoboken, NJ: John Wiley & Sons, Inc.

Sandmaier, M. (2017). 'Doorways to the Embodied Self: Eugene Gendlin and the Felt Sense.' *Psychotherapy Networker, 41:4*, 39–46

Van Der Kolk, Bessel, M. D. (2014). *The Body Keeps the Score*. New York, NY: Viking

HANDOUT 14.1: SENSORY WORDS RELATED TO ETHICS HANDOUT

acidic

antsy

bitter

coarse

comfortable

feverish

flaky

grounded

jittery

queasy

quenched

relaxed

restrained

rough

shaky

slick

slimy

soothing

strained

sticky

vibrant

HANDOUT 14.2: ETHICAL QUESTIONS RELATED TO TECHNOLOGY HANDOUT

1. Give an example of a breach of confidentiality when utilizing technology.

2. What is an example of a compelling professional reason to conduct an electronic search of a client without prior consent?

3. How might a professional website post cause a client harm?

4. How can you assure confidentiality when utilizing electronic communication?

5. What might be an inappropriate multiple relationship on social media?

6. What course of action do you take if you breach confidentiality when utilizing technology?

7. What course of action do you take if your online psychotherapy session is cut off?

8. Explain how posting personal information on your professional website might cause boundary confusion.

9. How might the delivery of electronic services be culturally insensitive?

ETHICAL QUESTIONS RELATED TO TECHNOLOGY
HANDOUT (P. 2)

10. Give an example of boundary confusion in digital communication.

11. Name a possible challenge for a client that might arise when using technology in receiving services.

12. How can you assess a client's capacity to provide informed consent for receiving services through technology?

13. What course of action do you take if you identify unethical professional conduct on social media?

14. How do you verify the identity of your client when utilizing technology?

15. Is it ethical to conduct an electronic search of your client?

16. Explain the ethical reasons for knowing the location of clients when utilizing technology to provide services to them.

17. What laws are pertinent when utilizing technology in the provision of services to a client in another jurisdiction?

18. How might technology improve access to services for people from vulnerable backgrounds?

19. How might online text-based interventions be modified for people with low levels of literacy?

20. What are some potential complications for a client who consents to post a positive comment on the professional website of a service provider?

Chapter 15

The Many Faces of Ethics

Making Masks

Objectives of Training

1. Identify cultural beliefs and biases conflicting with current Ethical Codes
2. Identify healthy ways to manage anxiety when faced with an ethical dilemma
3. Outline an ethical decision-making model
4. Articulate the ethical identity portrayed in a collaged mask

Description of Training

The Many Faces of Ethics: Making Masks uses mask making to explore the internal and external images we present to the world. In this mask making training, the internal and external images participants create will focus on their professional ethics personas. Each person has an internal image of themselves which they often do not share with others.

In mask making, we portray this internal image on the inside of our masks referring to it as our shadow or repressed side. The outside of the mask is designed with the image of ourselves we want others to see; this is our successful professional persona. Participants are guided through a series of journal prompts to explore the external face they present professionally as compared to their internal world. Each participant is given a mask to paint and collage on the outside and inside depicting this presentation. Various ethical issues and dilemmas are presented to continue an in-depth consideration of ethical conduct.

Intended Audience

Students, mental health professionals, other professionals, clients, and organizations
Suitable for individuals, small, and large groups

Approximate Time Suggested for Training

5 hours

Materials Suggested for Training

Copy of an applicable Professional Code of Ethics for each participant

Pre-shaped papier-mâché masks for each participant (These can be purchased at crafts stores or online. Papier-mâché masks are recommended rather than plastic masks because they are easier to glue and paint)

Paint, paint brushes, water containers, paper towels, markers, crayons, and Mod-Podge water-based sealer

Collage materials: colorful magazines, old books, catalogs, professional journals, feathers, buttons, beads, and an old book on ethics to cut up the words and text

Paper, pens, and pencils (participants are encouraged to bring their own journals)

Large sheets of newsprint paper to cover the tables

Provide soft music of various genres during the mask making, if desired

Handouts

List of Handouts

Contemplative Ethical Questions Handout #1

Ethical Case Dilemma Handout #1, *The Case of Facial Facades*

Contemplative Ethical Questions Handout #2

Ethical Case Dilemma Handout #2, *The Case of the Face Jordan Presents to the World*

Adaptations

Other professionals may substitute applicable Ethical Case Scenarios

For clients, modify handout questions and Ethical Case Scenarios to fit client specific issues

Procedures

1. Introductions, and review the objectives of the training. (10 minutes)

2. Explain that there will be silence as participants individually complete the Contemplative Ethical Questions Handout #1. Distribute the handout to all participants and instruct them to answer the questions on the form or in their own journals. Inform them that their answers will not be shared with anyone and will be kept private. Allow enough time for each participant to complete the five questions. (15 minutes)

3. Instruct participants to put aside their writing material and sit comfortably in their chairs with their feet on the floor and their hands gently relaxing in their laps. Read the following guided imagery out loud, very slowly. (5 minutes)

   - *Relax comfortably in your chair with your feet on the floor. Breathe deeply and feel grounded and safe in your surroundings. If you are comfortable, close your eyes gently. Imagine you are sorting through a small pile of unopened mail and you notice an envelope with your licensing board's return address. Notice your initial reaction. Do you notice a fight, flight, or freeze reaction? Just be aware of your reaction without doing anything else. Keep the envelope closed for the moment. Notice any sensation you have in your body.*

   - *Take three deep breaths, inhaling and exhaling completely. Fully relax your body and stay grounded and safe in your surroundings. Imagine that in the envelope is an official notice from your professional licensing board alerting you to a complaint against you, which is being investigated. Imagine the details of the complaint registered against you. What are these details?*

   - *Notice your reaction to these details.*

   - *How do you feel about yourself?*

   - *Notice what you want to do.*

   - *Take another deep breath in and out. As you take another deep breath you look closer at the letter. You notice that the letter is not addressed to you. The board has made an error and the letter is intended for another professional. Take another deep breath.*

   - *Notice your reaction to this realization.*

   - *Notice what happens in your body.*

   - *Notice your thoughts.*

   - *Allow yourself to accept the fact that this letter is not intended for you. When you are ready, open your eyes and breath gently.*

4. Instruct participants to write down all that they can remember of the guided imagery. They can write this on the back of the handout or in their journals. Inform them that their answers will not be shared with anyone and will be kept private. Allow enough time for each participant to write down their experience. (15 minutes)

5. Discuss with participants the idea that people present to the world an image of themselves that they want others to see. Each person also has an internal image of themselves which they often do not share with others. In mask making, we portray this internal image on the inside of our masks referring to it as our shadow or repressed side. The outside of the mask is designed with the image of ourselves we want others to see; this is our successful professional persona. In this mask making training, the internal and external images participants create will focus on their professional ethics personas. (5 minutes)

6. Give each participant a papier-mâché mask, and pencil. Instruct them to write some of the words and sentences from their handout or journal on the inside of the mask. These words will all be covered up and no one will ever see them. (5 minutes)

7. Instruct the participants to paint the inside of their mask a color of their choosing. (10 minutes)

8. While the paint is drying on the inside of the masks, instruct the participants to gather into small groups and to move their chairs into a circle. Once everyone is settled, distribute Ethical Case Dilemma Handout #1, *The Case of Facial Facades,* and read it out loud. (20 minutes to read and answer the questions in small groups)

Abby is a psychotherapist working in an addictions recovery program. Another therapist, at the program, Bonita, has been on emergency medical leave for six weeks. Abby has been assigned to pick up Bonita's caseload without a salary or benefit increase. Abby has a friendship outside of work with Bonita. Prior to being granted leave, Bonita told Abby that a mutual professional friend was going to falsify her medical records to substantiate the need for a medical leave. Bonita admitted she was trying to open a recovery program and wanted the time off to develop the program.

Abby's daughter, LaKisha, knows her mom has been stressed and working a double caseload. LaKisha gave Abby the gift of a 90-minute facial at a local spa to relax and take some time for herself. While getting her facial, the esthetician, Sondra, asks Abby questions to understand the reasons she is stressed. Abby tells Sondra that she is a psychotherapist and has been covering the caseload of a colleague for six weeks and is feeling overwhelmed. Abby is thoroughly enjoying her facial, especially the collagen facial mask. As they continue to talk, Abby tells Sondra the name of the program where she works and admits that she has fanta-

sies of quitting because she is so stressed and feels she is not doing good work. Sondra shares that her partner, Reginald, is receiving services at the same program and has been complaining of the long absence of his psychotherapist, Bonita.

- *Discuss in your small groups the following questions, referring to your Professional Code of Ethics when necessary:*
  - *At the point when Abby makes the connection between Reginald and Sondra, what should she do?*
  - *What does Abby do with the knowledge of Bonita asking another professional to falsify her medical records?*
  - *What does Abby do with the knowledge of Bonita taking time off to develop a recovery program rather than to recover from her own illness?*

9. Instruct participants to return to their masks and begin gathering the supplies they would like to collage onto the inside of the mask. Point out the various collage materials and remind them that the inside of the mask represents their dark or shadow side as a professional. This is the image they want to hide from others. Prompt them to refer to their written answers on the Contemplative Ethical Questions Handout #1. Explain they will have 15 minutes to gather their materials and start the process of collaging their mask in silence (with music playing in the background, if desired). After 15 minutes (while participants continue to work on their masks) the trainer will lead a discussion of the questions from the Ethical Case Dilemma which were discussed in the small groups. Keep this discussion going throughout the remainder of the time they work on the inside of their masks and ask for other ethical dilemmas participants might want to discuss. (60 minutes)

10. Monitor the progress of each individual's mask making, asking if they have questions or need some guidance. Give prompts as to how much time is left for the inside of the mask and explain that this can be a work in progress, not needing to be completed during the training.

11. Instruct participants to put their masks to the side and clear a space in front of them. Explain that there will be silence as participants individually complete the Contemplative Ethical Questions Handout #2. Distribute the handout to each participant and instruct them to answer the questions on the form or in their own journals. Inform them that their answers will not be shared with anyone and will be kept private. Allow enough time for each participant to complete the five questions. (15 minutes)

12. Instruct participants to put aside their writing material and sit comfortably in their chairs with their feet on the floor and their hands gently in their laps. Read the following guided imagery out loud, very slowly. (5 minutes)

Relax comfortably in your chair with your feet on the floor. Breathe deeply and feel grounded and safe in your surroundings. If you are comfortable, close your eyes gently. Imagine you have just taken personal time off from work and you feel rested and renewed. You turn on your phone and notice a voicemail from a trusted colleague or supervisor. You take a deep breath and listen to the voicemail. Your trusted colleague or supervisor compliments your recent decision and actions regarding an ethical dilemma you discussed with him/her. This person thanks you for being a positive role model and an inspiration to him/her. Stop the voicemail at this point.

- *Notice your reaction to this voicemail.*
- *How do you feel about yourself?*
- *Notice what you want to do.*
- *Take another deep breath in and out. As you take another deep breath you start the voicemail again. Your colleague/supervisor is naming positive qualities and traits which they admire in you. They thank you for all you add to the world and hang up.*
- *What positive qualities and traits do they admire in you?*
- *Notice your reaction to these words.*
- *Notice what happens in your body.*
- *Notice your thoughts.*
- *When you are ready, open your eyes and breath gently.*

13. Instruct participants to write down all that they can remember of the guided imagery. They can write this on the back of the handout or in their journals. Inform them that their answers will not be shared with anyone and will be kept private. Allow enough time for each participant to write down their experience. (15 minutes)

14. Instruct them to write some of the words and sentences from handout #2 or journal on the outside of the mask. These words will all be covered up and no one will ever see them. (5 minutes)

15. Instruct the participants to paint the outside of their mask with a color of their choosing. (10 minutes)

16. While the paint is drying on the outside of the masks, instruct the participants to gather into small groups and to move their chairs into a circle. Once everyone is settled, distribute Ethical Case Dilemma Handout #2, *The Case of the Face Jordan Presents to the World,* and read it out loud. (20 minutes to read and answer the questions in small groups)

Jordan has been a clinician for eight years in the local hospital emergency room since completing graduate school. His job requires him to complete clinical assessments and make appropriate referrals. He is planning to leave this job and open up a private practice specializing in working with couples and families.

- *Discuss in your small groups the following questions, referring to your Code of Ethics when necessary:*
  - *Is it ethical for Jordan to list couples and families as a specialty?*
  - *Jordan's marketing plan includes announcing his new practice to all the contacts on his phone and computer. What ethical concerns should Jordan be aware of when accepting referrals from these contacts?*

17. Instruct participants to return to their masks and continue working on the outside of their mask. Remind them the outside of the mask represents the image we want others to see – this is our successful professional persona. Prompt them to refer to their written answers on the Contemplative Ethical Questions Handout #2. Explain they will have 15 minutes to gather their materials and start the process of collaging their mask in silence (with music playing in the background, if desired). After 15 minutes (while participants continue to work on their masks) the trainer will lead a discussion of the questions from the second case dilemma which were discussed in the small groups. Keep this discussion going throughout the remainder of the time they work on the outside of their masks and ask for other ethical dilemmas participants might want to discuss. (60 minutes)

18. Monitor the progress of the individual participants' mask making, asking if they have questions or need some guidance. Give prompts as to how much time is left for the outside of the mask and explain that this can be a work in progress, not needing to be completed during the training.

19. Instruct participants to gather as a group in a circle for show and tell. Allow each participant to decide how much detail they want to share and if they want others to look closely at their mask. Encourage them to describe what they learned about themselves during this process and what, if anything, they want to change or add to their ethical identity. (20 minutes)

20. Ask for final questions, comments, and closing statements. (5 minutes)

Bibliography

Abels, S. (2001). *Ethics in Social Work Practice: Narratives for Professional Helping*. Denver, CO: Love Publishing

American Association for Marriage and Family Therapy. (2015). *Code of Ethics (PDF File)*.

Retrieved from www.aamft.org/iMIS15/AAMFT/Content/Legal_Ethics/Code_of_Ethics

American Counseling Association. (2014). *ACA Code of Ethics*. Retrieved from www.counseling.org/knowledge-center/ethics

American Mental Health Counselor Association. (2015). *Code of Ethics*. Retrieved from http://connections.amhca.org/viewdocument/amhca-code-of-ethics

American Psychological Association. (2017). *Ethical Principles of Psychologists and Code of Conduct*. Retrieved from www.apa.org/ethics/code/

Corey, G., Corey, M., & Corey, C. (2018). *Issues and Ethics in the Helping Professions, Tenth edition*. Stamford, CT: Brooks/Cole Cengage Learning

Koocher, G. P., & Keith-Spiegel, P. (2016). *Ethics in Psychology and the Mental Health Professions: Standards and Cases, Fourth Edition*. Oxford, UK: Oxford University Press

Knapp, S. J., Gottlieb, M. C., Handlesman, M. M., & VandeCreek, L. D. (eds). (2012) *APA Handbook of Ethics in Psychology*. Washington, D.C.: American Psychological Association

National Association of Social Work (N.A.S.W.). (2017). *Code of Ethics*. Retrieved from www.socialworkers.org/About/Ethics/Code-of-Ethics/Code-of-Ethics-English

National Board for Certified Counselors (N.B.C.C.). (2013). *Code of Ethics*. Retrieved from www.nbcc.org/Ethics/CodeOfEthics

Pope, K. S., & Vasquez, M. J. (2016). *Ethics in Psychotherapy and Counseling: A Practical Guide*. Hoboken, NJ: John Wiley & Sons, Inc.

Reamer, F. G. (2018). *Social Work Values and Ethics, Fifth Edition*. New York, NY: Columbia University Press

Strom-Gottfried, K. (2016). *Straight Talk About Professional Ethics, Second Edition*. Oxford, UK: Oxford University Press

Tribe, R., & Morrissey, J. (eds) (2015). *Handbook of Professional and Ethical Practice for Psychologists, Counsellors and Psychotherapists, Second Edition*. New York, NY: Routledge

Welfel, E. (2015). *Ethics in Counseling & Psychotherapy, Sixth Edition*. Boston, MA: Cengage Learning

HANDOUT 15.1: CONTEMPLATIVE ETHICAL QUESTIONS
HANDOUT #1

1. What are some negative emotional reactions you have about culturally diverse clients?

2. What biases and preconceived notions can you identify that you have regarding culturally diverse clients?

3. How might these biases effect you and your clients?

4. What fears do you have regarding your professional life?

5. Can you identify any personal beliefs you hold which might conflict with your Ethical Code?

HANDOUT 15.1A: ETHICAL CASE DILEMMA HANDOUT #1: THE CASE OF FACIAL FACADES

Abby is a psychotherapist working in an addictions recovery program. Another therapist at the program, Bonita, has been on emergency medical leave for six weeks. Abby has been assigned to pick up Bonita's caseload without a salary or benefit increase. Abby has a friendship outside of work with Bonita. Prior to being granted leave, Bonita told Abby that a mutual professional friend was going to falsify her medical records to substantiate the need for a medical leave. Bonita admitted she was trying to open recovery program and wanted the time off to develop the program.

Abby's daughter, LaKisha, knows her mom has been stressed and working a double caseload. LaKisha gave Abby the gift of a 90-minute facial at a local spa to relax and take some time for herself. While getting her facial, the esthetician, Sondra, asks Abby questions to understand the reasons she is stressed. Abby tells Sondra that she is a psychotherapist and has been covering the caseload of a colleague for six weeks and is feeling overwhelmed. Abby is thoroughly enjoying her facial, especially the collagen facial mask. As they continue to talk, Abby tells Sondra the name of the program where she works and admits that she has fantasies of quitting because she is so stressed and feels she is not doing good work. Sondra shares that her partner, Reginald, is receiving services at the same program and has been complaining of the long absence of his psychotherapist, Bonita.

- Discuss in your small groups the following questions, referring to your Professional Code of Ethics when necessary:
  - At the point when Abby makes the connection between Reginald and Sondra, what should she do?
  - What does Abby do with the knowledge of Bonita asking another professional to falsify her medical records?
  - What does Abby do with the knowledge of Bonita taking time off to develop a recovery program rather than to recover from her own illness?

HANDOUT 15.2: CONTEMPLATIVE ETHICAL QUESTIONS
HANDOUT #2

1. Describe how you feel emotionally and physically when you make a wise ethical decision.

2. Describe the thoughts you have about yourself when you make a wise ethical decision.

3. Which Ethical Values and Ethical Principles are most important to you?

4. What are healthy ways you manage your anxiety when faced with an ethical dilemma?

5. Describe your ethical decision-making process.

HANDOUT 15.2A: ETHICAL CASE DILEMMA HANDOUT #2: THE CASE OF THE FACE JORDAN PRESENTS TO THE WORLD

Jordan has been a clinician for eight years in the local hospital emergency room since completing graduate school. His job requires him to complete clinical assessments and make appropriate referrals. He is planning to leave this job and open up a private practice specializing in working with couples and families.

- Discuss in your small groups the following questions, referring to your Professional Code of Ethics when necessary:
  - Is it ethical for Jordan to list couples and families as a specialty?
  - Jordan's marketing plan includes announcing his new practice to all the contacts on his phone and computer. What ethical concerns should Jordan be aware of when accepting referrals from these contacts?

Chapter 16

The Grain of Truth

Enacting Ethics Through the Use of Sand Trays

Objectives of Training

1. Identify ethical issues related to multiple relationships and diversity
2. Describe the difference between healthy boundaries, boundary crossings, and boundary violations.
3. Symbolically represent an ideal ethical identity

Description of Training

The Grain of Truth: Enacting Ethics Through the Use of Sand Trays is a novel approach to studying ethics experientially. Using sand trays individually and as a group, this training guides participants to integrate ethical decision making from the symbolic to the actual.

Intended Audience

Students, mental health professionals, other professionals, clients, and organizations
Suitable for individuals, small, and large groups

Approximate Time Suggested for Training

4 hours

Materials Suggested for Training

Copy of an applicable Professional Code of Ethics for each participant
One large sand tray for each ten participants (and an additional large tray and trainer for each ten people)
Individual sand trays for each participant
A wide range of sand tray miniatures, objects, and small items (cotton balls, toothpicks, shells, stones, small hearts, etc.)
Sanitary hand wipes and paper towels
Paper and pens (participants are encouraged to bring their own journals)
Provide instrumental music during the activities, if desired (it is important to not have music with words)
Handouts

List of Handouts

Ideal Ethical Identity Handout
Sand Tray Guided Imagery Handout
Ethical Case Dilemma Handout, *The Case of Clinicians Putting Their Heads in the Sand*

Adaptations

Other professionals may substitute applicable Ethical Case Scenarios
For clients, modify handout questions and Ethical Case Scenarios to fit client specific issues

Procedures

1. Introductions, and review the objectives of the training. (10 minutes)
2. Explain the following terms:
   - *World* means the symbolic representation of the situation depicted in the sand tray.
   - *Miniatures* are the figures, toys, and objects used to create the world in the sand tray.
3. Explain that the first activity will involve all the participants creating a sand tray together. Each participant will choose a sand tray miniature depicting their ideal ethical identity. Then all participants will gather around the large sand tray and each person will place their miniature in the sand tray. The decision on where and how to place the miniature in the sand tray will depend on individual spatial boundaries and directional preference. This activity is an interactional, continuous process in which participants may choose to move their miniature as the sand tray world changes. Explain that the entire activity will take place in silence and participants are encouraged to keep their attention focused on the sand tray. Ask participants to not make eye contact with others or to make gestures. The activity will be concluded with a group consensus which will be signified by stillness in the sand tray. Before beginning the exercise, ask participants if they have questions or need clarification. (10 minutes)
4. Invite participants to choose their miniature and begin the activity. (15 minutes)
5. Once there is stillness in the sand tray invite participants to process the experience verbally while continuing to gather around the sand tray. Ask each participant to describe the meaning behind their chosen miniature. (20 minutes)
6. Instruct participants to be seated and distribute the Ideal Ethical Identity Handout. Explain that they can answer the questions on the handout or in their journals. (10 minutes)
7. Distribute to each participant an individual sand tray. Instruct them to depict the world according to their answers from the handout. Explain that this activity will also take place in silence. Before beginning the exercise, ask participants if they have questions or need clarification. Once all questions have been answered, invite participants to get up and choose the miniatures to begin the activity. (15 minutes)
8. Ask participants to share their thoughts on how this activity relates to making an ethical decision and "knowing" what to do? (10 minutes)

9. Instruct participants to clear their sand trays, return the miniatures, and set aside their writing material. Invite them to sit comfortably in their chairs with their feet on the floor and their hands gently relaxing in their laps. Explain that the following guided imagery involves the medical emergency of a loved one and allow participants time to ready themselves for possible intense emotions. Explain that after the guided imagery is read, they will be given instructions to be followed in silence. Although it might be tempting, encourage participants to keep their focus on their own world and avoid communicating with anyone else in the room. When everyone is prepared, read the following out loud, very slowly. (10 minutes)

Relax comfortably in your chair with your feet on the floor. Breathe deeply and feel grounded and safe in your surroundings. If you are comfortable, close your eyes gently. Imagine that during your work day you are notified a loved one has been rushed to the hospital and admitted to the Intensive Care Unit. Take three deep breaths. Imagine yourself taking actions to get to the hospital as soon as possible. What do you have to take care of at work to be able to leave and get to your loved one's side? Continue your deep breathing as you imagine making arrangements to leave and then travel to the hospital.

Imagine you are at the hospital. As you walk down the hallway of the ICU to the room of your loved one, continue your deep breathing. Now you are next to your loved one in the ICU. Emotions and questions begin to flood your mind. There is no one in the room except you and your loved one, who cannot yet speak.

You hear someone entering the room and you look up. You realize it is the doctor. You also realize the doctor is your client.

Continue your deep breaths. When you are ready, open your eyes and depict this world in your sand tray. Remember to focus on your own world and avoid communicating with others in the room. If you need support, please reach out to me.

10. Participants will now work on depicting their world from the guided imagery. The trainer gently supports everyone in remaining silent. (15 minutes)

11. Distribute the Sand Tray Guided Imagery Handout and instruct participants to answer the questions on the form or in their own journals. (10 minutes)

12. Ask participants who are willing to share their experience to explain what they learned from the process (showing their sand tray if desired). Discuss as a group the Ethical Case Dilemma and possible choices. (15 minutes)

13. Ask for a volunteer willing to share their sand tray which will necessitate allowing the group to make changes in it. Instruct the group to gather around the volunteer's sand tray. (5 minutes)

14. Ask for ideas of how a boundary crossing might be depicted with miniatures moved or added. Discuss all the ideas and then lead the group in a decision-making process of choosing one idea. Instruct the group to change the sand tray to depict the boundary crossing. (10 minutes)

15. Continuing to look at the sand tray, ask for ideas of how a boundary violation might be depicted with miniatures moved or added. Discuss all the ideas, and then lead the group in a decision-making process of choosing one idea. Instruct the group to change the sand tray to depict the boundary violation. (10 minutes)

16. Ask for ideas on a plan of action for dealing with the boundary violation depicted in the sand tray. Discuss all the ideas, and then lead the group in a decision-making process of choosing one idea. Instruct the group to change the sand tray to depict an Ethical Action Plan. (10 minutes)

17. Instruct participants to clear their sand trays, return the miniatures, and be seated. Distribute the Ethical Case Dilemma Handout, *The Case of Clinicians Putting Their Heads in the Sand*. Read the handout out loud. (5 minutes)

18. Instruct participants to stand up and gather around the large sand tray. Instruct them to depict the world of the case. (10 minutes)

19. Distribute a copy of the applicable Professional Code of Ethics to each participant. Discuss the ethical issues in this case. (10 minutes)

20. Instruct participants to view the sand tray from either eye level or from below looking up at it. This will necessitate sitting on the floor or kneeling down. Discuss how this view changes their perspective on the situation. Discuss how this relates to diversity issues. (10 minutes)

21. Instruct participants to view the sand tray from a distance. Discuss how this view changes their perspective on the situation. Discuss how this relates to diversity issues. (10 minutes).

22. Ask for ideas of how this ethical dilemma might be resolved. Discuss all the ideas, and then lead the group in a decision-making process of choosing one idea and changing the sand tray to depict the resolution. (10 minutes)

23. Ask for final questions, comments, and closing statements. (10 minutes)

Bibliography

Corey, G., Corey, M., & Corey, C. (2018). *Issues and Ethics in the Helping Professions, Tenth Edition.* Stamford, CT: Brooks/Cole Cengage Learning

Koocher, G. P., & Keith-Spiegel, P. (2016). *Ethics in Psychology and the Mental Health Professions: Standards and Cases, Fourth Edition.* Oxford, UK: Oxford University Press

Knapp, S. J., Gottlieb, M. C., Handlesman, M. M., & VandeCreek, L. D., (eds). (2012) *APA Handbook of Ethics in Psychology.* Washington, D.C.: American Psychological Association

Levitt, D. H., & Moorhead, H. J. H. (eds) (2013). *Values & Ethics in Counseling: Real-Life Decision Making.* New York, NY: Routledge

Pope, K. S., & Vasquez, M. J. (2016). *Ethics in Psychotherapy and Counseling: A Practical Guide.* Hoboken, NJ: John Wiley & Sons, Inc.

Reamer, F. G. (2012). *Boundary Issues and Dual Relationships in the Human Services, Second Edition.* New York, NY: Columbia University Press

—— (2018). *Social Work Values and Ethics, Fifth Edition.* New York, NY: Columbia University Press

Strom-Gottfried, K. (2016). *Straight Talk About Professional Ethics, Second Edition.* Oxford, UK: Oxford University Press

Tribe, R. & Morrissey, J. (eds) (2015). *Handbook of Professional and Ethical Practice for Psychologists, Counsellors and Psychotherapists, Second Edition.* New York, NY: Routledge

Welfel, E. (2015). *Ethics in Counseling & Psychotherapy, Sixth Edition.* Boston MA: Cengage Learning

HANDOUT 16.1: IDEAL ETHICAL IDENTITY HANDOUT

1. Describe the process of choosing a miniature to represent your ideal ethical identity.

2. Describe your reasoning of where to place the miniature considering spatial boundaries and directional preferences.

3. Describe what you experienced as others placed and moved their miniatures around the sand tray.

4. How did you "know" the placement of your miniature was in its final place?

5. How does this activity relate to making an ethical decision and "knowing" what to do?

HANDOUT 16.2: SAND TRAY GUIDED IMAGERY HANDOUT

1. Describe your thoughts when you realized the doctor was your client.

2. Describe your feelings when you realized the doctor was your client.

3. Describe how you decided to depict your world in the sand tray.

4. As you moved from choosing the miniatures to creating the world of this situation, what did you notice about yourself?

5. Look at the world you created in your sand tray. Do you notice anything you weren't aware of previously?

HANDOUT 16.3: ETHICAL CASE DILEMMA HANDOUT: THE CASE OF CLINICIANS PUTTING THEIR HEADS IN THE SAND

Polly is a recent M.S.W. graduate and accepted a full time job as a psychotherapist at the community mental health center (Sandybottom Services). Prior to graduation, Polly owned and operated a daycare center out of her home. Polly's daughter, Chloe, now runs the daycare from her mother's home.

Stasha, L.C.S.W. is the Clinical Director at Sandybottoms and is Polly's Clinical Supervisor. Stasha is married to Ronnie who is the stay at home parent for their four-year-old son, Maurie. One week ago Ronnie was in a car accident necessitating a lengthy hospitalization.

Derrick, L.C.S.W., is also psychotherapist at Sandybottoms and is also supervised by Stasha. He was given a written warning six months ago for engaging in inappropriate multiple relationships with a client. Currently Derrick is behind in his paperwork.

Polly asked to consult with Derrick about a personal matter. She asked him if he had any advice on behavior techniques to use with a four-year-old boy who is hitting and biting other children in her daycare. She explained that she doesn't know the boy very well because he has only been there a couple of days. Derrick gave her some suggestions including talking to the boy's parents.

Immediately after this conversation, Derrick overheard Polly speaking on the phone with her daughter (Chloe) about the behavior of a boy named Maurie.

Chapter 17

Ethical Sculptures

Objectives of Training

1. Identify a list of Ethical Values
2. Represent an Ethical Value without words using modeling clay

Description of Training

Ethical Sculptures is an expressive arts activity using clay modeling to explore ethics. Participants will identify a list of Ethical Values in a group discussion. Then they will choose one Ethical Value and form a representation of it by modeling clay. A handout provides questions for participants to reflect upon and answer. Finally, a group sculpture will be made representing an Ethical Value using Virginia Satir's experiential intervention of family sculpting.

Intended Audience

Students, mental health professionals, other professionals, and organizations
Suitable for individuals, small, and large groups

Approximate Time Suggested for Training

1 hour

Materials Suggested for Training

Modeling clay, paper towels, and hand-wipes (place in front of each participant)
White board or flip chart and markers
Handouts

List of Handouts

Ethical Sculpture Questions Handout

Adaptations

To extend the length of the training, additional clay representations can be made depicting ethical issues or dilemmas
To extend the length of the training, additional group sculptures can be completed depicting ethical issues or dilemmas
For client groups, substitute the word "ethical" with the word "moral"

Procedures

1. Invite participants to begin playing with the clay, which has been placed on the paper towel in front of them. Explain that you would like them to explore the clay by pinching, stretching, rolling, squashing, and/or pounding it during the following discussion.

2. Introductions, and review the objectives of the training. (5 minutes)

3. While participants continue to play with their clay, ask them to list Ethical Values which come to mind. Write these Ethical Values on the white board in the front of the room. (5 minutes)

4. Instruct participants to make a representation with their clay of an Ethical Value. Explain that there will be silence for the next 10 minutes as they mold their Ethical Value representation in the clay. Ask if there are any questions. The trainer will move quietly about the room quietly during this time, offering support or guidance as needed. (10 minutes)

5. Distribute to participants the Ethical Sculpture Questions Handout. Instruct them to complete the handout in silence. (5 minutes)

6. Instruct participants to find a partner, take turns, and share their Ethical Value representations with one another. (5 minutes)

7. Ask participants if anyone wants to share briefly their experience with this exercise and what they learned from it. (5 minutes)

8. Explain that the next exercise will be a group live sculpture which is an adaptation from Virginia Satir's experiential intervention of family sculpting. Ask for one participant to come to the front of the room and share their answer to question #4, describing the meaning of their Ethical Value representation in one or two sentences. Ask for volunteers to come to the front of the room and sculpt this representation as a group sculpture. They will place their bodies metaphorically in relation to one another while depicting the sentence description of the Ethical Value. (5 minutes)

9. Discuss with all the participants their response to this exercise. Ask them the following questions. (10 minutes)
   - *What have you learned about Ethical Values from this group sculpture?*
   - *If you were a volunteer in this group sculpture, in what ways did you practice ethical decision making while participating in this exercise?*
   - *If you were an observer, what did you learn about Ethical Values by watching the process of the group creating the sculpture?*

10. Ask for final questions, comments, and closing statements. (5 minutes)

Bibliography

Atkins, S., & Snyder, M. (2018). *Nature-Based Expressive Art Therapy: Integrating the Expressive Arts and Ecotherapy.* Philadelphia, PA: Jessica Kingsley Publishers

Congress, E., Black, P., & Strom-Gottfried, K.(eds). (2009). *Teaching Social Work Values and Ethics: A Curriculum Resource.* Alexandria, VA: CSWE

Koocher, G. P., & Keith-Spiegel, P. (2016). *Ethics in Psychology and the Mental Health Professions: Standards and Cases, Fourth Edition.* Oxford, UK: Oxford University Press

Levitt, D. H., & Moorhead, H. J. H. (eds) (2013). *Values & Ethics in Counseling: Real-Life Decision Making.* New York, NY: Routledge

Reamer, F. G. (2018). *Social Work Values and Ethics, Fifth Edition.* New York, NY: Columbia University Press

Satir, V. (1983). *Conjoint family therapy, Third Edition.* Palo Alto: Science and Behavior Books

Welfel, E. (2015). *Ethics in Counseling & Psychotherapy, Sixth Edition.* Boston MA: Cengage Learning

HANDOUT 17.1: ETHICAL SCULPTURE QUESTIONS HANDOUT

1. What Ethical Value does your clay represent?

2. How does your clay represent this Ethical Value?

3. What thoughts regarding this Ethical Value did you have while playing with the clay?

4. Describe the meaning of this Ethical Value representation in one or two sentences.

Chapter 18

Creating Ethical Super Powers

Objectives of Training

1. Describe potential ethical misuses or abuses in the power dynamic between professional and client

Description of Training

Creating Ethical Super Powers is a fun approach to learning ethics. A clip from the animated film, *The Incredibles,* sets the stage for participants to create an Ethical Super Power. The workshop combines an expressive arts exercise with discussions on the potential ethical misuses or abuses in the power dynamic between professional and client.

Intended Audience

Students, mental health professionals, other professionals, clients, and organizations
Suitable for individuals, small, and large groups

Approximate Time Suggested for Training

1 hour

Materials Suggested for Training

The Incredibles, 2004 Disney Pixar animated film
White board or flip chart and markers
Drawing paper
Crayons, markers, or colored pencils

Adaptations

For client groups, substitute the word "ethical" with the word "moral"

Procedures

1. Introductions, and review the objectives of the training. (5 minutes)
2. Explain that the clip is from a 2004 animated superhero film, *The Incredibles*. The film follows a family of superheroes who are forced to hide their powers and live a quiet suburban life.
3. Show the clip from *The Incredibles* 00:00–2:10.
4. Ask participants to brainstorm a list of super powers and write these on the flip chart. (10 minutes)
5. Distribute drawing paper and crayons, markers, or colored pencils to participants. Ask them to choose one super power they wish they could embody in their professional work. Instruct them to depict this super power on the drawing paper. Explain that this will be a quick sketch to be completed in a few minutes. (5 minutes)
6. Instruct participants to turn over their paper and write words or statements describing how this super power could enhance their ethical conduct and decision making. (5 minutes)
7. Instruct participants to write words or statements describing how this super power could be ethically misused or abused. (5 minutes)
8. Instruct participants to find a partner, share their drawing, and discuss the ethical benefits and potential harms of using their super power in a professional setting. (10 minutes)
9. Discuss with the large group ways the power dynamic between professional and client can be ethically misused or abused. (10 minutes)
10. Ask for final questions, comments, and closing statements. (5 minutes)

Bibliography

Abels, S. (2001). *Ethics in Social Work Practice: Narratives for Professional Helping.* Denver, CO: Love Publishing

Corey, G., Corey, M., & Corey, C. (2018). *Issues and Ethics in the Helping Professions, Tenth Edition.* Stamford, CT: Brooks/Cole Cengage Learning

Koocher, G. P., & Keith-Spiegel, P. (2016). *Ethics in Psychology and the Mental Health Professions: Standards and Cases, Fourth Edition.* Oxford, UK: Oxford University Press

Levitt, D. H., & Moorhead, H. J. H. (eds) (2013). *Values & Ethics in Counseling: Real-Life Decision Making.* New York, NY: Routledge

Pope, K. S., & Vasquez, M. J. (2016). *Ethics in Psychotherapy and Counseling: A Practical Guide.* Hoboken, NJ: John Wiley & Sons, Inc.

Tribe, R., & Morrissey, J. (eds) (2015). *Handbook of Professional and Ethical Practice for Psychologists, Counsellors and Psychotherapists, Second Edition.* New York, NY: Routledge

Welfel, E. R. (2016). *Ethics in Counseling and Psychotherapy: Standards, Research, and Emerging Issues, Sixth Edition.* Boston, MA: Centage Learning

Using Media to Learn Ethics

Section Summary: Using Media to Learn Ethics

Visual learning engages participants in the process and aids memory retention while stimulating thoughtful ideas. Helping professionals often claim their preferred learning style is through observation. *Using Media to Learn Ethics* offers an opportunity for a group to view the same situation together and review what they observed. Clips from movies and TV shows are an effective means of presenting case studies to promote discussion amongst the group.

Chapter 19

The Ethics of In Treatment is training that makes use of clips from a provocative HBO series, *In Treatment*, about a therapist who faces ethical dilemmas in virtually each episode. Written exercises facilitate independent thought prior to discussions on ethical decision making and boundaries. The clips help to weave discussions of self-disclosure, use of supervision, multiple relationships, accepting gifts, countertransference, and multicultural issues into this training, which participants describe as memorable.

Chapter 20

Picture Perfect Ethics offers participants a chance to watch clips from the TV show, *Monk,* and the movie, *Prime,* and apply knowledge from their applicable Professional Code of Ethics to various ethical issues. The clips have been specially chosen to showcase issues of privacy, confidentiality, use of technology, conflicts of interest, and multiple relationships. Participants leave training with a clear picture of applying Ethical Standards to ethical dilemmas.

Chapter 19

The Ethics of *In Treatment*

Objectives of Training

1. Identify and use an ethical decision-making process
2. Examine the strengths and limitations of professional boundaries
3. Identify relevant Professional Code of Ethics Standards to protect the confidentiality of deceased clients

Description of Training

The Ethics of In Treatment makes learning ethics fun and engaging. Using film clips from the HBO series, *In Treatment*, participants are led through written exercises and discussions on boundaries, self-disclosure, use of supervision, multiple relationships, accepting gifts, countertransference, and multicultural issues.

Intended Audience

Students and mental health professionals
Suitable for individuals, small, and large groups

Approximate Time Suggested for Training

4 hours

Materials Suggested for Training

Copy of an applicable Professional Code of Ethics for each participant
Equipment to show films
HBO series *In Treatment,* Season 1
White board or flip chart and markers
Handouts

List of Handouts

The Ethics of *In Treatment* Decision-Making Handout
The Ethics of *In Treatment* Boundaries Handout

Adaptations

To shorten this training, limit the clips shown
To extend this training, add additional clips from HBO's *In Treatment.*

Procedures

1. Introductions, and review the objectives of the training. (10 minutes)

2. Explain that there will be silence as participants individually complete the The Ethics of *In Treatment* Decision-Making Handout. Distribute to each participant the handout and instruct them to answer the questions. Allow enough time for each participant to complete the questions. The trainer can circulate around the room and provide support and guidance as needed. (15 minutes)

3. Discuss with participants their responses to the handout. (15 minutes)

4. Summarize the HBO *In Treatment* series by reading the following description. (5 minutes)

   Paul Westin earned his Ph.D. in psychology at the New School in N.Y.C.. He has a private practice in his home office in Baltimore, M.D.. Paul, as he prefers to be called, is in his fifties and lives with his wife and three children. The HBO series was originally run as a five-nights-a-week program. Each episode focused on one patient who came to therapy every week on a specific day. The last session of the week was Paul's own supervision and/or psychotherapy with Gina. Some of the ethical issues in the clips involve Paul as a therapist. Other issues involve his own work with Gina, which vacillates between individual and couples psychotherapy, and supervision. Paul's personal life is depicted in the show, as well, which highlights countertransference issues in the life of a therapist. The series ran for three seasons and in this training we will watch clips from Season 1.

   It might be helpful to delineate the various characters from *In Treatment* and their relationship to one another on the white board for clarification.

5. Explain that the first clip of *In Treatment* depicts Paul Westin providing psychotherapy to Alex who is a fighter pilot traumatized by a recent mission in Iraq where he killed 16 innocent people. Alex has a near death experience after the mission while running 26 miles with a friend. Alex is married to Makala and they have a nine-year-old son, Roy. Alex has been referred to treatment by his commanding officer before he can return to work as a fighter pilot. This clip is from Week Seven of the show, which means seven weeks into treatment. Alex is getting ready to make the decision to fly once again. Notice the espresso machine at the beginning of the clip. Alex gave this as a gift to Paul earlier in the season because he did not like the coffee in Paul's office. Show the clip from Season 1, Disc 7, Alex, 0:00–8:58. (10 minutes)

6. Briefly discuss with participants their initial reactions to this clip before showing the next clip. (10 minutes)

7. Explain that the next clip comes later on in the same session. Show the clip from Season 1, Disc 7, Alex, 15:47–23:26. (10 minutes)

8. Instruct participants to divide into small groups and discuss how they would handle the direct question from Alex, "Tell me, what would you do if you were me?" Remind participants to refer to The Ethics of *In Treatment* Decision-Making Handout. (15 minutes)

9. Ask if any of the groups want to report back to the large group particulars from their discussion. (10 minutes)

10. Explain that there will be silence as participants individually complete the The Ethics of *In Treatment* Boundary Handout. Distribute the handout to each participant and instruct them to answer the questions. Allow enough time for each participant to complete the questions. (15 minutes)

11. Discuss with participants their responses to the handout. List each boundary identified on the white board. (15 minutes)

12. Explain that the next clip is from a session the following day showing Paul and his wife, Kate, in couples therapy with Gina. Over the season of *In Treatment*, Gina has been in the role of individual therapist for Paul, supervisor for Paul, and, now, couples therapist for Paul and Kate. In addition, Paul has developed strong feelings for his client, Laura. In the first episode of the show, Laura, his client, declares her love for Paul and he sets an ethical boundary with her. As the season progresses, though, he falters with this boundary. Paul and his wife, Kate, are now processing their marital relationship in lieu of this boundary crossing. Show the clip from Season 1, Disc 7, Gina, 19:37 – until the end. (10 minutes)

13. Instruct participants to divide into small groups and discuss the various boundary and countertransference issues from the clip. Remind them to refer to The Ethics of *In Treatment* Boundary Handout. (15 minutes)

14. Ask if any of the groups want to report back to the large group the particulars from their discussion. (10 minutes)

15. Explain that the next clip is from a phone call Paul makes to Laura, his client. Remember that Laura has admitted to being in love with Paul. In the last clip, Paul is faced with his own feelings towards Laura. To further complicate matters, during the season Paul's two clients, Laura (who is in love with Paul) and Alex (from the first clip), have started a physical relationship. Both Laura and Alex are married to different people. Paul is aware that Laura and Alex have been seeing one another. Show the clip from Season 1, Disc 8, Laura, 7:32–11:05. (5 minutes)

16. Discuss with participants the boundary issues that occur in this clip, asking the following questions. (20 minutes)

- *Are there any specific situations in which it is ethical to call one client to inform them of the death of another client?*
- *What ethical guidelines should we follow when making disclosures to clients?*
- *Did Paul follow these guidelines?*
- *If you were Paul's supervisor and he told you of this phone conversation with his client, what would be your response?*

17. Explain that the next clip takes place in Paul's office with Alex's father, Mr. Prince. It is the beginning of the session in which Paul is discussing the protocol of psychotherapy. Show the clip from Season 1, Disc 8, Alex, 0:00–1:43. (5 minutes)

18. Distribute to participants their applicable Professional Code of Ethics. Ask them to discuss the ethical guidelines regarding confidentiality and privacy after a client dies. Ask participants to find the relevant Standard in their Code of Ethics and discuss. (10 minutes)

19. Explain that the next clip occurs later during the session with Paul and Mr. Prince. Show the clip from Season 1, Disc 8, Alex, 15:43–25:53. (10 minutes)

20. Instruct participants to divide into small groups and discuss the ethical dilemmas presented in the clip. Direct them to pay attention to issues of confidentiality and multiculturalism in the context of the clip. (15 minutes)

21. Ask if any of the groups want to report back to the large group the particulars from their discussion. (5 minutes)

22. Ask for final questions, comments, and closing statements. (5 minutes)

Bibliography

American Association for Marriage and Family Therapy. (2015). *Code of Ethics (PDF File)*. Retrieved from www.aamft.org/iMIS15/AAMFT/Content/Legal_Ethics/Code_of_Ethics

American Counseling Association. (2014). *ACA Code of Ethics*. Retrieved from www.counseling.org/knowledge-center/ethics

American Mental Health Counselor Association. (2015). *Code of Ethics*. Retrieved from http://connections.amhca.org/viewdocument/amhca-code-of-ethics

American Psychological Association. (2017). *Ethical Principles of Psychologists and Code of Conduct*. Retrieved from www.apa.org/ethics/code/

Farber, B.A. (2006). *Self-Disclosure in Psychotherapy*. New York: The Guilford Press.

Knox, S., & Hill, C. E. (2003). 'Therapist Self-Disclosure: Research-Based Suggestions for Practitioners.' *Journal of Clinical Psychology/In Session, 59,* 529–540

Luepker, E. T. (2012). *Record Keeping in Psychotherapy and Counseling: Protecting Confidentiality and the Professional Relationship, Second Edition*. New York, NY: Routledge

Koocher, G. P., & Keith-Spiegel, P. (2016). *Ethics in Psychology and the Mental Health Professions: Standards and Cases, Fourth Edition*. Oxford, UK: Oxford University Press

National Association of Social Work (N.A.S.W.). (2017). *Code of Ethics*. Retrieved from www.socialworkers.org/About/Ethics/Code-of-Ethics/Code-of-Ethics-English

National Board for Certified Counselors (N.B.C.C.). (2013). *Code of Ethics*. Retrieved from www.nbcc.org/Ethics/CodeOfEthics

Pope, K. S., & Vasquez, M. J. (2016). *Ethics in Psychotherapy and Counseling: A Practical Guide*. Hoboken, NJ: John Wiley & Sons, Inc.

Sue, D. W., & Sue, D. (2016) *Counseling the Culturally Diverse: Theory and Practice, Seventh Edition*. New York: John Wiley & Sons, Inc.

Welfel, E. (2015). *Ethics in Counseling & Psychotherapy, Sixth Edition*. Boston MA: Cengage Learning

HANDOUT 19.1: THE ETHICS OF *IN TREATMENT* DECISION-MAKING HANDOUT

1. What are the steps to ethical decision making that you follow?

2. How do you handle making a quick decision during a therapy session when a client asks you a direct question, such as, "What would you do?"

3. How do you handle making a quick decision on whether to accept a gift from a client as they are handing it to you?

HANDOUT 19.2: THE ETHICS OF *IN TREATMENT* BOUNDARIES HANDOUT

1. Make a list of ten therapeutic boundaries you hold (include physical and digital boundaries).

2. What are the strengths of the boundaries you hold?

3. What are the limitations of the boundaries you hold?

Chapter 20

Picture Perfect Ethics

Objectives of Training

1. Identify Professional Code of Ethics Standards related to privacy, confidentiality, and technology
2. Identify ethical choices when faced with conflicts of interest and multiple relationships

Description of Training

Watching popular TV and movie clips and then discussing the ethical issues presented stimulates learning. Clips from the TV show, *Monk,* and the movie, *Prime*, which pertain to a variety of ethical issues and dilemmas are shown. Participants are led through a discussion on ethical responses for each clip while referring to their applicable Professional Code of Ethics. Discussion questions focusing on client documentation; technology; termination; and multiple relationships, are included in the chapter.

Intended Audience

Students and mental health professionals
Suitable for individuals, small, and large groups

Approximate Time Suggested for Training

3 hours

Materials Suggested for Training

Copy of an applicable Professional Code of Ethics for each participant
Equipment to show films
Monk, TV Show, Season 5: Episode #7
Prime, movie with Meryl Streep

Adaptations

To shorten this training, limit the clips shown
To extend this training, add additional TV or movie clips

Procedures

1. Introductions, and review the objectives of the training. (10 minutes)
2. Summarize the TV show, *Monk*, by reading the following description: (5 minutes)

   Mr. Monk is a private detective and consultant for the San Francisco Police Department in the homicide unit. He used to work full time for the department until he suffered a nervous breakdown after his wife was murdered. He has a diagnosis of OCD with numerous phobias which cause him considerable distress yet allow him to see patterns and make connections while investigating a murder scene. His therapist is Dr. Kruger and Mr. Monk has been in treatment for many years with this psychiatrist. Episode #7, "Mr. Monk Gets a New Shrink" is from Season 5 of the TV show.

3. Explain that the first clip is of Mr. Monk and another patient arriving at Dr. Kruger's office at the same time for their individual appointments. Show the clip from 00:00–2:37.
4. Discuss with participants ethical responses for a therapist in this circumstance. (15 minutes)
5. Explain that the next clip is when Mr. Monk has been called in as a consultant to the murder at Dr. Kruger's office. Show the clip from 6:25–8:30.
6. Ask participants to refer to their Professional Code of Ethics and cite an applicable Ethical Standard for the following two questions. (15 minutes)
   - *What is the ethical action for the clinician if a client removes their file without permission?*
   - *What is the ethical responsibility if the clinician breaches client confidentiality and mistakenly sends a client's electronic file to a non-authorized party?*
7. Explain that the next clip is during the police interrogation of Dr. Kruger regarding the murder of his cleaning woman. The clip continues as Dr. Kruger informs Mr. Monk that he is going to retire. Show the clip from 8:30–13:40.
8. Discuss with participants their reaction to Dr. Kroger's response to the police interrogation. Have participants refer to their Professional Code of Ethics and cite an applicable Ethical Standard for the appropriate action in this situation. (15 minutes)
9. Discuss with participants their reaction to the manner in which Dr. Kroger announced his retirement to Mr. Monk. Ask the question, "*What are the ethical guidelines to consider when announcing retirement to clients?*" (10 minutes)

10. Explain that the next clip shows Mr. Monk arriving unannounced at the home of Dr. Kroger. Show the clip from 19:24–21:06.

11. Ask participants to refer to their Professional Code of Ethics and cite applicable Ethical Standards for the following questions. (20 minutes)
    - *What ethical guidelines should we follow if a client arrives unannounced at our home?*
    - *What are ways a client might invade our privacy?*
    - *What ethical guidelines should we follow to maintain privacy on web sites, social media, and other forms of technology?*

12. Summarize the movie, *Prime,* by reading the following description. (5 minutes)

    Meryl Streep is a therapist, Lisa, in Manhattan. Her client, Rafi, is a recently divorced, 37-year-old woman who becomes romantically involved with David. Over time, Lisa (the therapist) comes to the realization that Rafi's new love is Lisa's son.

13. Explain that the next clip takes place when the therapist (Lisa) has the realization that her client (Rafi) is dating her son (David). After ending the session, Lisa goes to her own therapist to discuss the situation. Show the clip from 27:40–31:02.

14. Discuss with participants various ethical responses to this specific situation of the therapist learning that the client is dating her son. (10 minutes)

15. Discuss with participants their reaction to the decision Lisa and her own therapist make regarding what to do. Have participants refer to their Professional Code of Ethics and cite applicable Ethical Standards for the appropriate actions in this situation. (15 minutes)

16. Explain that the next clip occurs when Lisa is out shopping with her husband and sees her son with her client. The scene progresses to the next therapy session and concludes with Lisa talking to her son about the situation. Show the clip from 55:05–1:01:00.

17. Discuss with participants various ethical responses to seeing clients in public. (10 minutes)

18. Instruct participants to refer to their Professional Code of Ethics and cite applicable Ethical Standards for the appropriate actions for the following questions. (20 minutes)
    - *What ethical guidelines apply to this clip regarding multiple relationships?*
    - *What should the clinician say and do with her client?*
    - *What should the clinician say and do with her son?*

19. Ask for final questions, comments, and closing statements. (5 minutes)

Bibliography

American Association for Marriage and Family Therapy. (2015). *Code of Ethics (PDF File)*. Retrieved from www.aamft.org/iMIS15/AAMFT/Content/Legal_Ethics/Code_of_Ethics

American Counseling Association. (2014). *ACA Code of Ethics*. Retrieved from www.counseling.org/knowledge-center/ethics

American Mental Health Counselor Association. (2015). *Code of Ethics*. Retrieved from http://connections.amhca.org/viewdocument/amhca-code-of-ethics

American Psychological Association. (2017). *Ethical Principles of Psychologists and Code of Conduct*. Retrieved from www.apa.org/ethics/code/

Farber, B. A. (2006). *Self-Disclosure in Psychotherapy*. New York, NY: The Guilford Press

Knox, S., & Hill, C. E. (2003). 'Therapist Self-Disclosure: Research-Based Suggestions for Practitioners.' *Journal of Clinical Psychology/In Session, 59*, 529–540

Luepker, E. T. (2012). *Record Keeping in Psychotherapy and Counseling: Protecting Confidentiality and the Professional Relationship, Second Edition*. New York, NY: Routledge

Koocher, G. P., & Keith-Spiegel, P. (2016). *Ethics in Psychology and the Mental Health Professions: Standards and Cases, Fourth Edition*. Oxford, UK: Oxford University Press

National Association of Social Work (N.A.S.W.). (2017). *Code of Ethics*. Retrieved from www.socialworkers.org/About/Ethics/Code-of-Ethics/Code-of-Ethics-English

National Board for Certified Counselors (N.B.C.C.). (2013). *Code of Ethics*. Retrieved from www.nbcc.org/Ethics/CodeOfEthics

Pope, K. S., & Vasquez, M. J. (2016). *Ethics in Psychotherapy and Counseling: A Practical Guide*. Hoboken, NJ: John Wiley & Sons, Inc.

Sue, D. W., & Sue, D. (2016) *Counseling the Culturally Diverse: Theory and practice, Seventh Edition*. New York, NY: John Wiley & Sons, Inc.

Voshel, E. H., &Wesala, A. (2015). 'Social Media and Social Work Ethics: Determining Best Practices in an Ambiguous Reality.' *Journal of Social Work Values & Ethics, 12:1*, 67–76

Welfel, E. (2015). *Ethics in Counseling & Psychotherapy, Sixth Edition*. Boston MA: Cengage Learning

Appendix 1

Blank Cards Handout

About the Author

Dayna Guido, MSW, LCSW, ACSW, is a psychotherapist, clinical supervisor, consultant, educator, and trainer. She has a private practice in Asheville, North Carolina, and specializes in providing clinical supervision for individual clinicians, groups, and organizations. Dayna's extensive range of supervision includes private practice, community mental health, wilderness therapy, residential care, and schools.

Living life creatively is a passion for Dayna and she brings this approach to her trainings. She has developed a wide assortment of clinical trainings which help the participant engage in the learning process. Dayna is a dynamic trainer whose provocative approach stimulates the learner to take the material, analyze it, and then incorporate it into their own practice. *Creative Ways to Learn Ethics* is a selection of ethics trainings, successfully offered.

She has been teaching graduate school for over 20 years as an adjunct instructor for Lenoir-Rhyne University, Clinical Mental Health Counseling, Asheville Graduate Center; University of North Carolina at Chapel Hill School of Social Work, Asheville MSW Distance Program; and ETSU, Department of Social Work, Asheville MSW Program.

Dayna is the co-author of *The Parental Tool Box for Parents and Clinicians.* She serves on the NASW-NC Chapter Ethics Committee. She can be reached at daynaguido.com.

Index